D0368738

PLAYING THROUGH

7/00   Andy —
        We've enjoyed
watching you grow
and our friendship
your 1st 18 years of
life. Here's to
continued friendship
and may you
enjoy "Playing Through"
your life.
            the Freys

Also by Earl Woods

Training a Tiger (with Pete McDaniel)

PLAYING THROUGH

Straight Talk on
Hard Work, Big Dreams
and Adventures with Tiger

EARL WOODS

with Fred Mitchell

Foreword by
Tiger Woods

HarperCollins*Publishers*

HarperCollins books may be purchased for educational, business, or sales promotional use. For information please write: Special Markets Department, HarperCollins Publishers, Inc., 10 East 53rd Street, New York, NY 10022.

FIRST EDITION
Designed by Irving Perkins Associates

Library of Congress Cataloging-in-Publication Data
Woods, Earl, 1932–
        Playing through : straight talk on hard work, big dreams, and adventures with Tiger / by Earl Woods with Fred Mitchell ; foreword by Tiger Woods. — 1st ed.
        p.   cm.
        Includes index.
        ISBN 0–06–270222-X
        1.   Woods, Tiger. 2. Woods, Earl, 1932– . 3. Golfers—United States—Biography. 4. Fathers and sons—United States. 5. Racially mixed people—United States—Biography. I. Mitchell, Fred. II. Title.
        GV964.W66A3 1998   98–5607
        796.352'092—dc21   CIP
        [B]

98 99 00 01 02 RRD/❖ 10 9 8 7 6 5 4 3 2 1

This book and its pages are dedicated to the memory of my departed friend and wartime comrade Colonel Vuong Dang Phong, known to most of the world as Tiger Phong or the original Tiger. Our paths met and merged for the briefest period of time but resulted in fond memories full of heartbreak that will last a lifetime. He was my counterpart and fellow soldier but above all my friend. It saddens me to know that he starved to death lonely and tortured in an infamous Vietnamese "re-education" camp to which he had been sentenced after the war as a "war criminal." In my heart he was a soldier, patriot, and hero. And I will carry his tragic loss to my grave.

CONTENTS

ACKNOWLEDGMENTS

. . . .

I wish to publicly thank a few key people who contributed so unselfishly to the completion of this project of love: Shari Wenk, literary agent, who worked so hard yet whose sunny disposition made it so pleasant; Patty Leasure, Greg Chaput, John Atkins and the rest of the staff at HarperCollins, whose dedication and effort far exceeded expectations or requirements; Fred Mitchell, writer, whose patience and sensitivity captured the true essence of my work; Tom Callahan, writer for *Golf Digest,* to whom I will always owe a debt for investigating and bringing to closure the true fate of Tiger Phong. To all of you, and the many others that contributed, you have my heartfelt thanks and gratitude.

FOREWORD

By Tiger Woods

My life has been an open book, at least in golf circles, from the time I was old enough to swing a golf club. Although much has been written on my golfing career, this book is the first extensive biographical examination of my life beyond the camera's eye. There is more to Tiger Woods than fairways and greens—and who better to share this with you than my father who has been there at every step of the way.

When I was growing up, my parents loved to remind me that I was named Eldrick (my birth name) for a special reason. The "E" at the beginning represents Earl and the "K" at the end stands for Kultida. My mother said she wanted their initials to encompass my name so that I would always be surrounded by my parents. Thankfully, that has been the case. So much of who I am comes from my parents. Although I am an only child, my mother and father never spoiled me. I am the product of their careful guidance and discipline, which hopefully helps bring out the best in me. The many ideals and lessons I've learned from my mother and father define who I am and make me proud of who I am. Their unwavering trust and confidence in me keep me going each day.

Pop wears many hats in our relationship. He is my counselor, my coach, my conscience, my inspiration, and my hero.

He is an invaluable, indispensable, and irreplaceable player on "Team Tiger." Without his friendship, guidance, and support, I would not be where I am today, and last year would have been more than somewhat daunting.

Pop has always challenged me to be the best I could be in all areas of my life. By his words and actions, he has been and continues to be my role model for pushing my own limits and reaching higher levels, both on and off the golf course. The title of his book comes from this defining trait of my father, a trait which I hope I can emulate in my own life. Throughout his life, he has had the fortitude and determination to be the best he could be in spite of resistance at so many steps along the way. In *Playing Through*, he shares some very personal childhood memories and experiences over the course of his life in the hope that we can all learn from them. This book will make you think about your own abilities, your desire to achieve certain goals, and your determination to face challenges and overcome obstacles.

As you can imagine, 1997 was an amazing year for me for many different reasons, and it tested my own abilities to "play through." Growing up on the PGA tour is an exhilarating, trial-and-error experience. In a relatively short period of time, I have learned an awful lot about the game of golf and about myself. I learned that I can compete with the best golfers in the world. At the same time, I came to appreciate what it takes to maintain the high level of performance that is demanded at each tournament stop. It gives me great comfort and peace of mind to know that my dad is with me at a tournament, and he gave me quite a scare last year with his heart surgery and lingering heart ailments. It's times like these when we're reminded of our own mortality and appreciation of others.

People often ask me what my goals are for golf. Suffice it to say, winning the Masters Tournament in 1997 was one of them. I know that repeating this in 1998 will be an even more daunting task; however, I am way too young to rest on my laurels and current ranking among golfers. Staying on top is more difficult than getting there—and most people would agree that it is better to be "in the hunt" than to be "the hunted." I know everyone will be gunning for me, and that's just fine—Pop taught me everything I need to know about 'playing through.'

As much as I crave winning every tournament that I enter, the most important lesson my father taught me is that the ultimate mission in life should go beyond the playing field or the golf course. "Share" and "care" are two words you'll come across over and over again in this book, just as I've heard them from my father throughout my life. This message is the inspiration for the Tiger Woods Foundation, a non-profit group that my dad and I founded. We feel it is extremely important to give back to the community and to support programs that can promote wholesome ideas for our world's young people.

By reaching out to kids in previously ignored inner-city locations, the Tiger Woods Foundation continues to change the face of golf to include more minorities and younger people. With the help of a growing network of individuals and agencies, the word is getting around that we're on the right track. I am more proud of my involvement with the Tiger Woods Foundation than any tournament I've ever won. Through the game of golf, we're able to spread the good word about sportsmanship, family relationships, education, and solid values—building blocks that will make our world a better place.

My father and I make a great team, and I try to tell him as often as I can that I love him, not only on Father's Day, but every day. No one in this world knows me better than my dad, and I trust him here to tell our story with the same diligence, pride, passion, and straight-shooting that have become his hallmark.

Happy Father's Day, Pop

INTRODUCTION

· ·

THE GAME OF GOLF can be a metaphor for life. My life, for certain. I have experienced my share of birdies and a few eagles, yet it seems I have encountered more sand traps and bogeys than I care to recall. With every obstacle or challenge I've faced, however, I've managed to work through it and come out stronger and wiser. And as I walk down the 18th fairway of my lifetime, I hold my head high and make no apologies for the decisions and statements I have made. I realize now that everything happens for a reason, that there is a plan for all of us, which includes both good times and bad. The more astute among us are able to learn from our misfortunes and become stronger individuals. I have been a survivor, a living testimony that others like me can beat the odds, withstand the cruelties, indignities and setbacks that life can offer. I certainly hope the experiences I'll share in these pages will serve to motivate others to press on when the going invariably gets tough.

For those of you who play golf, you already know the sport's definition of "playing through." And using golf as a metaphor for life, the term playing through takes on a broader, more powerful meaning. Playing through means getting down to business, not letting anything get in your way, dealing with the task at hand, accomplishing your goals, not getting distracted by things that don't really matter, knowing yourself and drawing on that sense of self to get you through difficult times. *Playing Through* is my story, and, correspondingly, the story of Tiger.

When Tiger and I celebrated his stunning Masters victory by embracing, the television image was seen by 15 million people. President Clinton called it "the best shot of the day." I also have heard it called "the hug felt around the world." This hug was an unspoken symbol of our mutual respect and an acknowledgment of all that goes into accomplishing a goal. In the pages that follow, you will find many stories about myself and about Tiger—the bricks in the foundation that helped to build and reach these dreams.

My intention in writing this book is to bring people together, not set them apart. At times, I may speak from the seat of my pants, but I also speak from my heart. Those who know me well will affirm that I am not averse to showing my sentimental, compassionate side. I am not afraid to let people see me cry. But I have had a few close calls with meeting my maker, and I just don't seem to have the patience anymore to always say things perfectly or diplomatically. If I sound terse and irascible, it's because I simply, finally, want to be heard.

Along with the accolades and adulation Tiger has received during his relatively brief rise in the international spotlight have come criticisms and accusations—most of them totally unfounded and malicious in spirit. I have had my share of detractors, as well. While I do not feel compelled to answer to anyone except myself, I also believe, in another sense, that it is incumbent upon me to set the record straight on many topics regarding Tiger's and my purpose and agenda. You see, ours is a bond that can and will withstand any bombardment of innuendo or jealousy. That is because we deal in truths and concerns for the human spirit. Armed with those solid weapons, we cannot be beaten down. Don't judge us until you know our story, until you know the nature of our life experiences.

The greatest misconception the public seems to have of me is that I am a dominating, possessive, dictatorial stage father. That is exactly 180 degrees from the truth. Some people have suggested that I forced Tiger to play golf and made him do this and made him do that. Some people have raised questions about my first marriage and my three children from that relationship. They have tried to sully my current marriage with rumors and speculation. They have dwelled on the fact Tiger did not win a tournament in the second half of 1997, instead of emphasizing the fact he had the greatest year by a rookie in PGA history. I address all of those topics in this book.

My whole life is about being positive. It's about dreaming, and then taking steps in your life to achieve those dreams. It is about overcoming obstacles and stereotypes such as bigotry and prejudice. Life is about giving and about sharing and caring for others, standing up and being counted for what you believe in, being a spokesperson and a role model, and being an inspiration.

The heart that will beat forever in my soul belongs to my youngest son, Tiger. He is the product, symbol and extension of my beliefs. My wife, Tida, says that he is "The Universal Child" and that Tiger represents everybody in the world because of his diverse ethnic makeup. The fact that he is one of the world's greatest golfers is relevant only to the extent that the game provides him an international forum and platform to espouse our beliefs, which quite simply could bring families and nations together.

I come from a family where love was a given. We stood by one another at every crisis and did the right thing. That was a greater expression of love and affection than hugs or words or tangible presents. Giving gifts on holidays is not a normal practice for Tiger and me, either. Our relationship is so deep and so powerful and so strong that it does not need validating with gifts. It is enough for us to share and celebrate the fact that we are one. We don't just celebrate on Father's Day; we do it all of the time, because everyday is Father's Day for Tiger and me. I wish that other parents would establish relationships with their kids so that every day would be Father's Day and Mother's Day, too, because that's what it is all about. You can't celebrate a relationship like that only once a year. You have to live it.

And when you live it, there is no gift that could honor that relationship, other than the gift of each other.

Although both of my parents died when I was young, they created a foundation and model for family relationships and interaction that will stay with me forever. I would say that 90 percent of that family training came from my mother, and the other 10 percent came from my oldest sister, Hattie, who ran the household after my parents died. My mother's lessons were so profound and so positive that they became deeply ingrained in my personality. Those lessons proved beneficial in raising Tiger, because I realized how important it was to instill these principles in a child at a very early age.

Relatively speaking, Tiger has not experienced a great deal of adversity in his life. Yet, almost by osmosis, he has felt the pain I endured, because I've shared the ignominy with him during many of the bedside talks that we had. The embarrassment of going to school with holes in your shoes; the taunts, snubs and personal and professional roadblocks based on race that I encountered. Tiger has experienced these feelings through me. Adversity can be transferred verbally, and the lesson is learned. Obviously, I did not have the desire for my son to go through the humiliations that I did. But I did want him to learn from the indignities that I experienced. Dealing with adversity and challenges has become a part of his character, and it is the lesson learned that Tiger can fall back on throughout his life, as I have done.

Tiger and I certainly do not profess to have all the answers, but I hope that our story will inspire people of all ages to rise to every occasion and to turn obstacles into opportunities. Life will always be a work in progress filled with unexpected twists and turns, and new joys and new challenges. But one thing is for certain: Tiger and I are determined to keep playing through.

LIFE LESSONS TO PASS ON

· ·

Chapter One

THE POWER OF FAMILY

WHEN I WAS a youngster in the 1930s, the focal point of our family's entertainment was the colossal radio in the living room of our unpretentious dwelling at 1015 Yuma Street in Manhattan, Kansas. In my mind's eye I still can see that mammoth Zenith. Back then, of course, there was no television; heck, we didn't even have a car or a telephone. On a typical hot summer night, our entire family gathered around that virtually living, breathing hunk of furniture with the booming, pulsating wire-mesh speaker where a heart should be. In the background an electric fan would be whirring while our imaginations were stirring amidst the static from the radio.

When it was "Fight Night" on the radio, nothing else mattered in the household of Maude and Miles Woods, especially when heavyweight champion Joe Louis entered the ring. We didn't even eat. Total attention was devoted to the magical box.

As I close my eyes and transport myself back to those simpler days, I can hear the staccato, play-by-play voice of legendary ringside announcer Don Dunphy: "And there's a right and a left by Louis! And Louis has knocked him down to the canvas! . . . two, three, four, five . . ."

Whenever Joe Louis would win yet another fight, all our neighbors would spill out into the street afterwards, screaming and cheering and talking about *our* heavyweight champion. He elevated the esteem of the entire black race: We all had a personal investment in how Joe Louis, the "Brown Bomber," fared. He was the heavyweight champion, the hero of the black people, the hope of the black people. He was our shining light.

Joe Louis happened to be a close friend of one of our neighbors, a Mr. Fred Harrison. On occasion, when Louis came to town, he would stay at Mr. Harrison's house. I can still see him dressed in his Army military uniform; he was stationed only eight miles away at Ft. Riley, Kansas. Louis loved children, and I distinctly remember meeting the Champ when I was a kid. Little did I realize then what lessons I was learning about the significance of sports heroes in our society, and how my very own son, Tiger, would assume a similar role a half century later.

I learned at that very early age that being a sports hero involved embracing certain important qualities and responsibilities. People were watching, learning, hanging on every word and deed. I vividly remember my mother saying to me then: "Don't you dare talk the way Joe Louis talks when you grow up! I want you to get an education, and I want you to speak properly."

Nothing was more important to my mother than education, and she was right. I believe today that my mother's lessons were unwittingly meant to someday guide me in raising Tiger. As you will see throughout this book, I deeply believe that some mystic power up above was preparing me to raise a son who would be articulate, intelligent and learned. I was so young when my mother was teaching me all of this—she died when I was only 13—but I followed her gospel, and many years later used it to guide my own son. This feeling of destiny and fate controlling our lives was introduced to me through my mother and her strong religious convictions, and my own belief in these ideas have only been enhanced by my own incredible life experiences.

I learned at a young age that when the door of opportunity opens, only those who are prepared will walk through before the door closes. As I've watched my youngest son stand in that doorway and leap through it with stunning grace and confidence, I've come to realize that every experience I've ever had, each hardship and each blessing, has been part of the great plan that brought me to this place in history. If I had lived a different life, could I have given Tiger the tools he would need to be an international star at age 21? Would I have had the insight to guide his God-given talents? Could I have prepared him for the pressure he would shoulder, the criticisms, bigotry and loneliness he would often be forced to confront? I truly believe that without the many obstacles I have faced in my own life—from poverty to racism to near-death in war—I could not have raised the son you see before you today.

When I reflect on the incredible and unlikely events that brought my family to this place and time, I recognize that my own background plays a tremendous and critical role in Tiger's history. Now, I realize that every parent is probably wondering, "Why does Earl think he's any different from other parents; don't all parents' pasts shape and influence how they raise their children?" Yes, this is true. What is truly out of the ordinary is my youngest son, and everyone wants to know what makes him tick—how did he become such an exceptional talent and inspiring role model. But in order to know Tiger, you need to understand some of the parenting that went into "the making of Tiger."

I was born in Manhattan, Kansas, March 5, 1932, the last of six children. I used to tell my sisters and brother that my parents had been searching for the perfect child and when I finally arrived, they said: "That's it. We finally got it." But I don't think they bought it.

I had four sisters: Hattie, Freda, Lillian and Mabel. My brother, Miles, was the oldest. All except Mabel are deceased now.

My sister Mabel and I pose for an early picture.

We were a proud family with strength of unity and conviction. Yet financial circumstances at the time often meant tremendous personal sacrifices. I am not proud of it, but I distinctly remember our family receiving Thanksgiving Day food baskets from the Rotary Club. But in my mind, we were not poor; I didn't grow up feeling inferior to anyone, at least not in my mind. Our personal worth remained rich and stable within the confines of our family, which was firmly headed by my mother.

Though I was young when my mother died, I remember vividly so many details about her. She was of average size with hair of an unusual off-gray tint. She was a very soft-spoken woman who minced no words. To be sure, she was very straightforward, honest, sincere and intelligent. She also had allergies that caused her to sniffle incessantly: I can remember every time she would come into the house, I would hear her sniffle, and that's how I knew she was home. It was unmistakable.

We lived in a wood-frame house with a prominent front porch. Originally, it had two bedrooms; later, another bedroom and bathroom were added. It also had a cellar where we stored all the food that Mom canned. In the fall, she canned blue plums and yellow cling peaches for the winter. She also canned string beans, corn, peas, rhubarb and pickled watermelon rinds, which were all stored down in the basement. I can still smell the wonderful aromas of that fruit when she was canning.

In the backyard, we had a walnut tree, grapevines and a pear tree. We also had beautiful flowers all around the house—a picturesque setting in an otherwise mundane neighborhood. We raised chickens in the backyard, and it was my job to pick

Me, at seven years of age, in my front yard with my new puppy Stinky at our home in Manhattan, Kansas.

out the chickens that we were going to eat. I raised them from the time they were baby chicks, and some of them were real feisty. I would go out there and get three of them and think nothing of doing what I had to do for the next family meal: grab them by their feet, swing them around until they got real dizzy, lay them on the ground, put my foot on their necks and pull their heads off. Mom would clean them. I was never squeamish about killing the chickens, even as a little boy.

On the left side of our house there was a huge tree, on which I nailed a backboard, so I could go out and shoot baskets. Everything we had in those days was makeshift, because there was no money to buy anything. The best Christmas gift I ever had as a kid was a 25-cent kite, with a tail I made from a rag and a ball of string I saved up from the newspaper wrappings. I was eight years old, and I was deliriously happy, running in the Kansas snow with my homemade kite. Our Christmas tree was decorated with only blue lights, because that was all we had. To this day, I love the color blue because of our tree.

What we lacked in luxuries we made up for in solid values. I was blessed with having a mother who could teach her children how to live. Even though she only lived until I was 13, she had a profound impact on me and created great direction in my life. My beliefs, my priorities, and the way I look at people and treat people . . . I didn't know it then, but these were implanted in me by my mother. She was a great woman.

My mother would not allow our circumstances to affect her wisdom and her philosophy of life, nor her aspirations for her children. She was a driving force who never stopped stressing the importance of good grades. She insisted we go to school every day, even in Kansas snowstorms when there would be three or four feet of snow on the ground. There was no such thing as missing school. "Get your education," she said, "because that's something no one can take away from you." My mother was a college graduate, but like many young black women in those days, she could not obtain employment consistent with her education. She ended up working as a maid for people who didn't have the education she did.

She set the standards in our house, and they were very high. The attitude manifested itself in me in that she would not tolerate mediocrity in anything I attempted. I learned to speak well. I learned to write well. She would always say that people need to be able to read what you write. Don't make it difficult for them. So penmanship was a very high priority with her. And she insisted on good grades.

But, like so many young kids, I tested my parents' boundaries. When I got a few *unsatisfactory*'s in conduct on my grade card—there was that impish side of me—Mom told the teacher: "Double his workload." That cured the problem. I never got an unsatisfactory in conduct after that, because I never had time to get into trouble. The deal was, when I finished my work (which had become an impossible task), I was free to play. I later used that philosophy in my military and leadership principles and in combat. My motto was and still is, "Work hard and play hard."

Above all, my mother had dignity and pride. She taught all of that to me and to my sisters, too. Pride in self. She didn't express it the way they do now, by saying "love yourself." Instead she used expressions such as "pride" and "you are responsible for your own actions." Those concepts have been the cornerstones of everything that I have done in my entire life, and the very essence of what I have tried to instill in Tiger. It comes from a deep sense of self. I love myself. I love who I am. I respect who I am. I need no outside validation of that through either material means or through the opinions of others. I know that I am a good person. I always have been a good person, and I always will be a good person.

These beliefs have made me pretty strong, since I am not at the mercy of the opinions of others. When you combine this with my strong sense of responsibility, you can see that I became a very serious person at a very early age. And I was able to survive many things that might have crushed someone else.

Although my father was a Baptist and my mother was Methodist, I had an opportunity to go to both churches; there was no pressure on me to choose one church over the other. I think that later made it very easy for me to respect the religion of my wife, Tida, who is Buddhist; we came to an easy understanding about how we would raise Tiger with both religions. The objective was that Tiger would have a choice. It seemed so natural and normal for me, because that is the way I was raised. There was no bickering, nobody saying, "This religion is better." The important thing was that we did go to church— and I loved to participate in church activities. Some of the most joyful times I had as a child were in the Christmas programs—I remember the hours I used to practice my presentations, because my mother was a perfectionist: "You *will* learn how to speak. You will *not* use lazy English."

From the beginning, it was so important to me to follow what my parents taught me and what they stood for. It wasn't so much that I wanted to please them, but that I wanted to do the right thing, to be a good person, and I felt that their teachings would lead me there. I found great satisfaction in doing what they said, because it was right. I think the same is true of Tiger today: He doesn't do things just to please his parents; he does what he thinks is the right thing to do. And if we have taught him well, he will do just that.

I did not identify my father as my saving grace. He was my teacher. He was not what you might call a "people person." He was not one to sit down and engage in philosophical talks with me. He just taught me the value of appreciating certain tangible things. My father taught me to appreciate the value of manual labor and the merit of work. I learned at an early age that there is no substitute for hard work. I never questioned that notion or had any reservations about rolling up my sleeves and getting down to basics.

My father was every bit as nurturing as my mother, but he had different goals for me. My father's ambition for me was to become a professional baseball player, specifically, a member of our homestate Kansas City Monarchs of the old Negro Leagues, a team that would later spawn future major league Hall of Famers such as Ernie Banks. He felt I had real talent, and I suppose it was true; I had a very, very strong arm and an instinct for the game.

Our family lived near a ballpark where an all-white team from the Ban Johnson League played their games. These were young men between the ages of 18 and 25. How ironic that an all-white team would come to our section of town, but not allow blacks to play. The only way we could get near that field was by the grace of the groundskeeper, who would allow our neighborhood team of black kids to practice there all morning long if we helped him drag the field and get it ready for the real game at night. My father was the full-time scorekeeper at the park. I would hang around outside the ballpark and chase foul balls, because you got a nickel for each returned ball. So my father was in the park keeping score and I was outside chasing foul balls. I always managed to take one ball home that my buddies and I could use for practice.

Because of my father's role as the official scorekeeper at that local baseball field, I also had access to the diamond when the Negro League teams came to town during their exhibition tours. I was allowed to be batboy for the Negro League team during those barnstorming tours two or three times each summer, watching players like Hall of Fame pitcher Bob Feller. Pretty incredible for a small Kansas boy with big dreams. The experience had a profound impact on me.

My father was a typical outdoors worker who toiled in masonry. He would come home wearing his overalls and the bib; I will never forget the buckles on the top, the little latches. He had this favorite silly little hat with a feather in it. He loved flowers, which seemed a contradiction to me: He taught me the sheer love of flowers and how to lay mason brick. What a combination!

Together, my father and I built a stone wall in front of our house where I grew up. He showed me how to select the proper stones and taught me the principles of support and cross-support. He also demonstrated to me how to mix mortar. . . . I will never forget. When I would mix a mortar, I would make it too dry, and Dad would say, "It needs some more water." Then he would spit in it. I thought that was awfully humorous. I would think: "That ain't much water." But I couldn't say that to him. That was just the way he chose to teach me about the proper amount of water in the mixture of sand cement to make this mortar. My father communicated to me the love of the outdoors and working with my hands, and to this day, I get a great deal of pride from working with my hands.

My father also taught me gardening. I love to work in the garden. I used to take a sick plant and with tender love and care nurse it back to health again. I always have had that knack. I was in charge of the family garden, and I learned at a very early age how to cut potatoes and plant them, and then take care of them and grow the whole garden. My mother would say: "Go out and get something for dinner tonight." I would go out and dig some potatoes, pull some radishes, cut some lettuce, pick some corn and get a couple of cucumbers. And for dessert I would pick a watermelon. Not only was there pride in doing that, but I enjoyed it. The simple little act of eating tomatoes that you have grown yourself and that have never been in the house . . . you just wipe 'em off, lick 'em, put a little salt on there and, boy, that is the best tomato you have ever eaten in your life.

I grew up in a hurry when I was eleven, after my father died suddenly of a stroke. By then, my older brother Miles had gone into the Air Force, and I was the only guy at home. I will never forget my father's funeral, where my mother put her arm around me in church and said, "Son, you're now the man of the house." That simple statement transformed my life. It changed me from being a freewheeling, totally happy-go-lucky kid into a responsible young man. I took those responsibilities seriously. As a result, responsibilities began to regulate my life.

The most painful thing for me was to watch my wonderful, dear mother literally grieve herself to death over the loss of my father. I remember her sitting there in her old oak rocking chair, humming to herself the hymn "What Are They Doing in Heaven Today?" Over and over and over again. She was so devastated by her loss that she lived only two years after his death; she died of a stroke, just as my father had. I was 13.

Strangely, my mother's funeral was not as traumatic for me as my father's had been, perhaps because I had already suffered the devastation of losing someone close to me, perhaps because I was a little older when she passed away. In addition, I suppose I knew intuitively that my mother's death was coming soon; her suffering was so deep and profound.

I was about to learn my first lesson about what it means to "play through." To be 13 years old and have no parents . . . it was terrifying, unthinkable. Suddenly there were distant family members everywhere—at the funeral, hovering around us— bickering in hushed voices about what should happen to us, the children of the late Maude and Miles Woods.

There was only one answer that would have suited my mother: We would not split up. So my oldest sister, Hattie, who was 29, stood up and said: "We are not going to be separated. We will stay here in this house. I will raise everybody." That is what happened, and I will be eternally grateful to my sister Hattie for becoming our surrogate mother. I owe her greatly.

After our parents died, we took care of ourselves and each other. My mother had instilled such strong beliefs and values in us that there was really no need for outside support or discipline. We still had a pretty close-knit family. Sure, there was some sibling rivalry between us. But the age difference between Hattie and the rest of us meant there was no real problem. Unquestionably, Hattie was in charge. She told us what we had to do. She gave us our chores, and it was just business as usual. We continued to do the things we were supposed to be doing. I had the garden and the yard to take care of; my sisters kept the interior of the house in order. I admit I took an attitude typical of "men" in that era: I insisted that I not do housework. I would not wash the dishes, for instance, because I felt then that the man of the house simply didn't do things like that. I was lucky that my sisters went along with it, since I did have plenty of other chores to do. But the arrangement shaped the way I am today: I could have 10 vacuum cleaners and I still wouldn't touch them. I know how that sounds, but it's what I am.

After our parents died, our family rallied around each other and supported one another in our various ventures. When I played American Legion baseball, for example, they would travel all over the state to all the games to watch me play. Hattie and her husband, Jesse Spearman, and all of my sisters would be in the stands. It wasn't always easy for them, because they would be the only blacks in the entire stadium. They endured a lot to be there to support me. As the catcher, I was right there in front of the whole crowd, an easy target for countless bigots who didn't hesitate to hurl the "n" word all the time, anytime. Yet my sisters and my brother-in-law had to be cool and composed amidst the racial slurs and other denigrating comments from the crowd.

No question, our ability to rise above it came from my mother, who instilled in us a strong philosophy about dealing with adversity. She always would say, "Treat others the way you would want to be treated: with respect and pride." Yet my mother never allowed racism to become a major topic in our home; we learned more from our experiences than we would from her teachings. But she emphasized being a good person— not being a good *black* person, but a good person. I have passed this on to Tiger, who has said many times, "I don't want to be the best black golfer, but the best golfer." That comes from my mother.

My high school class was comprised of mostly white kids; interestingly, Tiger would grow up the same way, surrounded by white friends. But unlike Tiger, when I was a boy, socializing with white girls was practically out of the question; interracial dating was unthinkable. And since there was only one black girl in my class, whom I didn't particularly like, my options were pretty limited. The closest thing I had to a girl-friend was a cheerleader, who happened to be white. She was one year behind me in school, and very attractive. We liked each other, but it was not permissible for us to be together publicly back in those days, so there was never any serious relationship. Even at school dances, interracial dancing was frowned upon. The best we could do was ride on my bike (with her on the handlebars) up to the Kansas State University tennis courts and play tennis up there.

At the end of my senior year, the school administrators found themselves in a tricky spot: I was a final candidate for King of the prom, which would be voted on by my classmates. Yet tradition held that the King would kiss the Queen, and, well, you can picture the mayhem that ensued when they envisioned Earl Woods kissing a white Queen. So the vote was rigged—by adults—so that I could not win. Yet those were the times.

I reached a true crossroads in my life when I graduated from high school. My mother's last wish was that I be educated, that I go to college. My father had always dreamed that I'd play professional baseball. Faced with the opportunity to do both, the decision was gut-wrenching.

I had received a scholarship to Kansas State—I was the only one in my family who received a scholarship to college, and that was to play baseball. Let's face it, blacks were not offered academic scholarships back then the way they are

In front of my house at 16 years of age. I told Tiger I had a 28-inch waist; now this is proof.

today. Why would you educate a black kid when you could educate a white kid, who could take his education and get a good job? What kind of jobs were waiting for college-educated blacks? So there was virtually no help available in terms of student loans. The only reason we were all able to go to college was we all lived at home. All we had to pay was tuition and books, which was difficult enough.

In the end, four of the six of us would become college graduates, an astounding feat for a poor family with no parents. When I look back on that accomplishment, I say: "That's not too bad, Mom, with you not being there."

Kansas State was about four miles from where I still lived with my family, and I rode my bicycle there every day. I will never forget that bike: It consisted of no more than two wheels, a frame, a handlebar and a seat. The absolute basics. It had those big, wide Texas Longhorn handlebars. And I would go peddling that bike into that cold, strong Kansas wind, all the way up to the university, tears rolling from my eyes as the wind howled. My hands were numb from the chill as my legs kept pumping my way to school. But there was no money to ride the bus, certainly none to buy a car.

It was a tough adjustment for me. I was still playing baseball—my real love—while trying (although not too hard) to do well at school. Baseball was winning: At one point, I almost got kicked out of school because I discovered you could actually cut classes without anyone getting on your case, a realization I took full advantage of . . . until I was placed on probation. You might call it the "Negative Dean's List," because I cut so many classes.

And then I was confronted by one of the biggest decisions I had ever faced. I was offered a contract from the Kansas City Monarchs. My home team, the team my father had loved and for whom I had been a batboy, had offered to make me a professional baseball player. It meant making my father's dreams come true—at the expense of my mother's dream that I get an education. I could drop my scholarship and play baseball, or continue with school. Couldn't do both.

The long, lonely night I had to make a decision was painful. I was so torn between the wishes of my late parents. I remember trying to reach out to them, soul-searching, spiritually, until I believed I could hear their voices telling me what to do. Dad had always wanted me to play baseball; I think he envisioned that baseball was the way to a better life. But my mother's ambitions for my education were so ingrained in me that they were almost written on my soul. To ignore her wishes was almost unthinkable.

My mother's voice of reason prevailed.

I majored in sociology and minored in psychology at Kansas State, and it has been psychology—along with 20 years of military service—that has forged my philosophies and thus

Tiger's mental discipline. Mental toughness and tempered optimism are survival techniques that blacks have adopted, historically. My mother instilled in us that nobody is going to give you anything, that you have to be better than others in order to get an equal chance, and I have found that to be true. So has Tiger. Yes, it is still true to this day.

I did continue to play baseball at the collegiate level, as my son would do in golf many years later. I broke a few barriers of my own, as the first African-American baseball player in the Big Eight Conference. Long before discrimination in sports would be a pivotal issue to Tiger, it was a way of life for me. His occasional experiences now hauntingly bring back to life what it was like being a pioneer. Both the glory and the ignominy—the pain and the exhilaration—of those years will remain indelibly etched in my memory. But my ability to withstand those hardships has served to help me teach Tiger how to deal with similar adversities as a pioneer on the PGA Tour, under a much harsher spotlight than I ever had to deal with.

Throughout those difficult years, I don't know what I would have done without my oldest sister, Hattie, a very wise and giving person who raised us under the most stressful of circumstances. Yet she graduated from college, and became an elementary school teacher. She subsequently met a returning veteran from World War II, Jesse Spearman, who would become the strong male figure in my life after my father died. Jesse was in the premed program at Kansas State University, and he and I became friends. After Hattie and Jesse got married, we became even closer friends. Our relationship literally changed my world; if not for him, my entire life would have taken a different direction.

Jesse had been a captain in the Army, and during World War II, he had sent home almost his entire salary to his brother, who was supposed to deposit it for Jesse; it was designated as money that would pay for Jesse's medical school when he returned from the service.

When Jesse finally came home from the war, he told his brother: "Let's go down and get the money out of the bank."

But his brother said, "There's no sense in going down there, because there is nothing in there." His brother had spent all of the money while Jesse was over there fighting. I learned a very important lesson that day.

So Jesse was faced with finding another way to finance his medical education, which he did. He had the dream of becoming a doctor, and eventually it was realized. He became a gynecologist.

When it came to having an older, responsible male figure to talk to through my young adult years, Jesse Spearman came through every time I needed him.

The night before I was to enroll for my junior year in college, Jesse sat down with me to talk about my future. He strongly recommended that I go into Advanced ROTC, which I was not planning to do. Carving out a career as a military officer was the farthest thing from my mind at that point of my life. I had already survived two years of basic ROTC, only because they were mandatory at Kansas State, and I was pretty negative about the experience. Also, I was under the impression that in order to become a military officer, you really had to be a genius—that you had to have straight A's in college, which was not the case with me.

Jesse and I kept talking and discussing late into the night, about the benefits and advantages of a military career, yet I felt pretty confident that was not the life for me. But the next morning, as I was on my way to enroll for my junior-year courses, something came over me. All of a sudden, inexplicably, I had second thoughts. I stopped in my tracks, as if redirected by some powerful external force, turned around and went over to the ROTC department.

I asked them if it was too late to get into Advanced ROTC. The representative said, "Yes, you should have decided months ago."

Then he said: "What's your name? Just a minute." I believe he recognized me because I was the school's only black ballplayer, not because I appeared to have any great future in the military.

He called the professor of military science: And I overheard the professor say, "What is his name?"

The representative said, "Earl Woods."

And the professor asked, "Is that *the* Earl Woods, the baseball player? Get him in the program."

So the department broke all the regulations, and I went into Advanced ROTC. Strange as it seemed then, that bizarre, unaccountable alteration in my thinking changed my entire life.

Nearly a half-century later, as I think about that fateful late-night conversation with Jesse Spearman, I keep thinking: Without it, there would be no Tiger. There would be no Tiger because I wouldn't have been in the military. We all have those moments when we realize that fate has played a tremendous role, and that was certainly one of mine, a defining moment of my life that makes me believe today that I was being prepared for something, that I was being selected by a higher power. The decision to stay in school and give up a professional baseball career with the Kansas City Monarchs, the choice to go into Advanced ROTC . . . without that, there would not be a Tiger.

I was not aware of it at the time. But it supports my belief that Tiger was brought here for a reason, that his purpose was planned by a higher power long before he was planned by his parents.

Were it not for my mother and her incredible sense of ethics and values, I doubt I would have had the ability to raise a son like Tiger. Above all, she always taught us not to hate people, not to judge. Her famous saying was, "There's a professional judge Upstairs, who makes no mistakes. Leave the judging to Him, and devote all your energies to living and helping other people. That will make your life more fulfilling."

Even though I signed up for the ROTC and turned down the chance to play professional baseball, I never gave up my love for the sport. This is me several years after graduation, coaching and playing for the WACOM Rhinos, my military baseball team in Kaiserlautern, Germany.

At crucial points during Tiger's career, I have gotten in touch spiritually with my sisters. Hattie was an avid Tiger fan. When she knew she was dying, she came to watch Tiger play as an amateur in the U.S. Junior World Championships in San Diego. She wasn't strong enough at that point to stand, so we had to bring a lawn chair for her to sit in. She was so proud of Tiger. And my second oldest sister, Freda, was an avid fan of Tiger's, too. She was dying of cancer when Tiger was just a little kid, and he and I took an emergency flight to Denver to see her. Tiger crawled up in the bed with her to hug her and say "I love you." It was a very touching moment. That was the same year that Tiger appeared on the television show *That's Incredible*. So we arranged for Freda to see Tiger's appearance on it.

In crucial moments since their deaths, I have talked with my sisters. I ask them: "Please, give Tiger support. He can use all of the help he can get. I know you are watching." And they always have been there. They hear my prayers.

• •

Chapter Two

PUSHING LIMITS AND BREAKING BARRIERS

AT TIMES, TIGER refers to me as a "tough old codger." I take that as a compliment. It is an earned and deserved moniker, the consequence of extensive military training that has enriched me with great mental and physical stamina. This training has also helped make Tiger into a pretty tough guy as well: He has surely benefited from the hard lessons I learned about durability, lessons that I know he carries with him onto the golf course and, more importantly, into life. From the time he was six months old, sitting in his high chair watching me hit golf balls into a net, it has been my 20 years of military service that have contributed mightily to Tiger's awesome capacity for mental discipline.

After graduating from Kansas State University and then playing semipro baseball while I waited my call to active duty, I joined the Army where I taught a variety of subjects including military history at City College of New York. Eventually I served two tours of duty in Vietnam. Yes, I have seen the face of death many, many times and it never gets easier. No question, it was the violence of war that shaped the rest of my life and influenced every priority for me.

Somewhere, in a dusty folder in an obscure file cabinet where military records are preserved, it is affirmed that I, Earl Dennison Woods, served in the Republic of Vietnam from February 12, 1962, to February 24, 1963, and again from August 15, 1970, to August 13, 1971. I first entered active military service in 1954, following graduation from Kansas State, and I retired with the rank of lieutenant colonel in 1974. Generally, I do not recall specific dates and times from my military career as much as I remember the fascinating people, remote locations, indescribable events and distinctive sights, sounds and smells; but these dates happen to be fresh in my mind from *Golf Digest* magazine's efforts to track down my friend in the service—Tiger Phong—after whom Tiger is named.

Ironically, military life was not the easiest thing in the world for me, because I am not your typical military-minded individual. A true military mind is task-oriented, sometimes to a fault: "Here is a job, get it done." I, on the other hand, am highly people-oriented. I care about the people doing the job. I took a management seminar for executives at Columbia University in New York during my service years, and my test results determined that my management style heavily emphasized people over tasks. I considered people to be more valuable than equipment, and I still do. So while the typical military mentality was to give orders, take orders and ask no questions, it was important to me that the people around me knew what and why certain assignments had to be performed. I felt I had to be honest with my men, rather than demanding they simply take orders from me. I went as far as to take suggestions from my subordinates, allowing input from everyone who cared to offer it. It was an unthinkable attitude—definitely not the military style of the '60s and '70s—and very unpopular with other officers. But that was my way, the best way I knew how to lead. I guess I was just ahead of my time.

In the beginning of my military career, I never dreamed I'd stay in the service as long as I did, or that it would become so central to my life. At the time, I was just taking notice that there were few career options for blacks, particularly in a city like Manhattan, Kansas. Young black men tended to go either into the military or to work in the post office, regardless of their level of education. It was also becoming painfully clear that any aspirations I still had about a baseball career were futile—the decision to stay at school instead of opting to play for the Monarchs had sealed that fate. And it was not an easy transition to make, shifting from prominent college athlete to the military. But like so many young men I knew—including my brother, Miles, who went into the Air Force after finishing his education—I decided the military might be the only way for me to go.

The service changed a lot of things for me. For one, I smoked my first cigarette after I joined the military, a habit I still struggle with today despite Tiger's constant campaign to help me quit. I started smoking, I think, when I finally realized that I was not going to become a career athlete. At that time, of course, it was so common to smoke—nobody was really aware of the long-term effects. So I said to myself: "I might as well enjoy myself a little bit more." I also took my first drink at the tender age of 22 years old, when I was a second lieutenant in Germany. When I was growing up, no beer or wine, no alcohol of any sort, had ever been allowed in our house. Nobody smoked. Nobody drank. It was all about school, work and, of course, church. But I wasn't perfect then, and I'm not perfect now.

If there was ever an example of playing through, it was my military career. No doubt, it was a very trying period in my life: I was constantly fighting racism, discrimination and lack of opportunities. There was just no chance for an intelligent, articulate black person to do anything worthwhile or participate successfully in the process of life. It was frustrating and suffocating in so many ways, particularly for someone who wanted to achieve things but wasn't given the opportunity. I was constantly thwarted—my superiors would not give me the conventional requisite assignments which would qualify me for subsequent promotions. For instance, I was not given the opportunity to be a unit commander in an infantry unit. Those went to the "regular" Army people and the West Pointers. I was a professional career assistant, with no path up the ladder.

Yet somehow, for some reason, I survived by playing through for twenty years. It chills me to think that if I had given up, if I had let the racists drum me out, I never would have met my wife Tida, and we would not have had Tiger.

My career nearly came to an abrupt end when I was a second lieutenant in the army, stationed in Germany, in a defining moment forever etched in my memory. A lieutenant colonel (who was white) called me into his office and said sarcastically, "Lieutenant Woods, how do you get your shoes to look so good?"

I looked him dead in the eyes and fired back: "A little bit of shoe polish and a whole bunch of elbow grease, sir."

Well, I don't know what the "proper" answer would have been, but that surely wasn't it. He was a redneck who was incredulous at my confidence, and he was furious that I would answer in such an impetuous, insurgent manner. He glared at me with contempt and said: "You stay right here, Lieutenant." He indignantly marched outside, excused the other officers in a nearby room and told them to take an early lunch. He didn't want any witnesses to what was about to happen. When he came back inside; I could almost see the steam billowing out of his ears. His mouth was twisted into a vicious snarl.

He squared off directly in front of me and blasted into my face: "You're one of those smart niggers. We don't have any place for people like you in the Army. I'm going to make damn sure that you don't stay!"

That was the beginning of the long, painful journey for me. When he wrote my efficiency report, he rated me a one on a scale of zero to seven. I knew that I was a good lieutenant and that I did not deserve this. My subsequent actions proved this to be true. But that was his way of getting back at me, and, in those days, there was no legal or military protection or recourse. He didn't have to show me the report or review it with me.

Actually, I never would have known about that report if it hadn't been for a black personnel sergeant who typed the efficiency reports and sent them to the Pentagon. He had the courage to secretly call my house to tell me what he had seen. "Sir," he said, "you had better get out of here. This guy has got it in for you."

So I began looking for another job in the command, but before I was able to transfer out, the vindictive colonel took his last shot at me—he had just enough time to issue one more report. This time, instead of a one, he gave me a zero. He wrote in the report: "This officer has absolutely no value to the military service."

That could have been the end for me. But my next superior officer issued a report that reflected my true abilities and performance, stating the exact opposite of what the previous colonel had written. An officer who reviewed my records with me years later in the Pentagon noticed the discrepancy and told me: "Somebody had it in for you. This report totally refutes the earlier one, but it's still going to cost you a promotion to captain."

So the spiteful, racist colonel achieved what he set out to do—throw what appeared, at the time, to be an insurmountable roadblock in the path of my military career. And, for a time, he succeeded. You see, I was not a West Point graduate, nor was I a so-called regular Army officer. I was a reserve officer with an ROTC commission source, which meant initially I got the third-rate jobs. I was assistant-this and assistant-that. In other words, I did all the work and other guys got all the credit. As a result, they moved on up the ladder much faster.

However, I was fortunate enough through the succeeding years to receive positive, accurate reports. I subsequently made captain and then major, which was a huge jump; I made that promotion on schedule. And I made lieutenant colonel on schedule. I was able to do a lot of good things, and I caught up to most of my peers in the military. I didn't fully catch up to everybody, though, but I made up for some lost time. The experience instilled in me a great feeling of pride and confidence. I was able to tell myself: "You have done your job." I was playing through.

In the end, I achieved something very critical and lasting: As a result of that appalling experience with the lieutenant colonel, I made a conscious decision and a social commitment to use my misfortune to affect positive change in the military from within the ranks. I took the challenge seriously. Wherever I went throughout the rest of my military career, I told my first-hand account of discrimination to other officers, black and white. I received individual promises and pledges from them, that when they achieved the appropriate rank, they would do something about the blatant bigotry and racist practices that were so in vogue during my early years in the service. I wanted their promises that they would rectify conditions, so this type of discrimination would never happen again. I had risked sacrificing my career to get this done, and I needed to know it wasn't for nothing.

Some of those guys are now two- and three-star generals, so I figure my efforts were worth the pain and indignation. Young black soldiers in the service today are treated far better than I ever was, and I hope my actions and those of other pioneering African-Americans years ago had something to do with that.

Ironically, it was discrimination that led me to the Green Berets. After years of fighting prejudice and unfairness, I had to take a hard look and ask myself: "Who will give me a fair chance?" I found my answer in the extraordinary world of the Green Berets. In this most specialized organizational unit, the *esprit de corps* extends all the way from the bottom to the very

One of my sergeants congratulates me on my promotion to major while in Korat, Thailand.

top: No one man is perceived to be better than the other. Each unit is like a chain, no stronger than the weakest link. You depend on each other, like you have never depended on anyone in your life. Respect, dignity, honor . . . it was what I had been searching for throughout my entire career. So, in 1967, at age 35, I went into the Green Berets, just to get that long-awaited fair shot.

As an ex-athlete, I wasn't intimidated by the rigorous training associated with becoming a Green Beret. In fact, I looked at it as a tremendous challenge. I completed the jump training school at Ft. Benning, Georgia, and was then assigned to the army's Special Warfare Center in Ft. Bragg, North Carolina, for qualifying school.

As the No. 1 ranking officer in the jump class at Ft. Benning, I was the class leader, expected to set an example for others. One frosty January morning, attired only in a T-shirt, fatigue pants, and spit-shined jump boots, we were starting physical training for the day, with pull-ups as the first exercise. There was a half-inch of ice on the pull-up bar, and we were not permitted to clean it off. As the class leader, I had to mount the bar first. No gloves were authorized. I can still feel my fingers on the ice, virtually sticking to the bar as I tried to elevate my chin over the barrier. It was agony.

Talk about playing through: Every day I was learning crucial lessons about what it really meant—and more importantly, what it took—to survive. On military runs, if a guy was having trouble, he would suddenly find two strong arms lifting him without losing cadence and keep right on running. In jump school, we ran every day. There were no quitters, no dropouts—not in my jump class, anyway.

Picture this: We're Green Berets attending the Arctic survival school in Alaska, with the temperature around minus-50 degrees, the winds blowing 40 miles an hour. Our mission: move cross-country about 20 miles through scrub oak. We had a team in front, hacking a path with razor-sharp machetes across the frozen tundra laced with scrub oak head high and thicker than dandruff. The rest of us were pulling a sled loaded with our equipment and supplies. We're deep into it when one guy collapses. "I just can't go any farther," he says.

I pulled up alongside the slumping soldier and said matter-of-factly: "You are going to die. They will come in next year, and they will find you standing here, frozen to death. Because if you think there is somebody who is going to bring a truck to pick you up, you are wrong. If you think anybody else is going to carry you, then you are wrong."

And we moved out. He caught up with us in about two miles. He had pushed himself to another level, a capacity he didn't even realize he had. Believe me, he was very, very happy to learn what he was capable of achieving. As a leader you do almost anything to motivate your men, even the weakest link, to perform. Everyone must carry his share of the load in the

Captain Woods, embarking on a cross-country trek while in frozen Alaska. I was there as a Green Beret while attending Arctic survival training. The temperature was –50 degrees Fahrenheit.

unit. Throughout each grueling exercise, each of us discovered how far we could push our minds and bodies under adverse conditions—lesson number one to be passed onto Tiger.

When I completed the training at Fort Bragg, North Carolina, I was qualified as a Green Beret commander. What an honor and feeling of accomplishment. At long last, I would be treated as an equal, and allowed to treat others as the same. I was electrified and privileged to be in a position to influence and lead young men's lives. What an elite group of soldiers they were.

Unlike most of my previous superior officers, I didn't lead by intimidation: I led by caring and by opening the lines of communication. My troops knew what we were doing and why. My mother used to say: "You can lead a horse to water, but you can't make him drink.". . . Well, my troops were there because they wanted to be there and they knew why. They always felt part of a team.

No task was too small for me. I can remember being inside a field kitchen stove with steel wool in my hands getting it ready for inspection. The guy next to me was a private. I was a major, his commander. But I was inside the stove just like he was, scrubbing away. That is how I earned the respect of my troops, by showing them that I was truly "one of them."

During the height of the Vietnam conflict, I was the briefing officer for the Vietnam village at Ft. Bragg, North Carolina, where John Wayne filmed the movie *The Green Berets*. I was stationed there while the movie was being made, and although I wasn't in the film, I sure did live the story after graduation and in subsequent tours in Vietnam.

Was I shot at? Sure, I was shot at just like everybody else. But being shot at during wartime is very impersonal. Scary, but impersonal. You are just another hunk of flesh wearing the wrong-colored uniform. You hear bullets flying, whizzing by your ear, and you're thankful to be hearing them, because it means they missed. You never hear the one that hits you. Thank God, I have never been hit by a bullet, although I had some very, very close calls.

The fact that I survived at all has only reinforced my belief that a higher power was protecting me. I'm sure I had a guardian angel on one shoulder, but I also had a true friend from the "here and now" watching my back. His name was Lieutenant Colonel Vuong Dang Phong. Maybe you know him by his other name: He is the original "Tiger," the man for whom my son is named.

There is nothing comparable to the comradeship you experience in wartime and on the battlefield. Perhaps the closest civilian experience might be found on the police force, between partners. But Tiger Phong and I, well, we were more than friends. We were like two brothers; the only difference was that brothers don't share bullets. We did. It was a beautiful relationship that crossed cultural backgrounds.

I was his adviser for a year, and Col. Phong was Deputy

Chief of Binh Thuan Province, Republic of South Vietnam. He commanded all Vietnamese military forces in the Province with headquarters in Phan Thiet. We would go into relocation hamlets where complete villages had been transplanted to so-called safe zones, and we could really feel the silent hatred and animosity toward us as we walked through the village streets. The Viet Cong had a bounty on my head, and on Tiger Phong's head as well. You never knew who was your enemy; you could never get behind those piercing, hate-filled eyes. I would look around at the people there and know in my heart that I could be looking directly into the eyes of a Viet Cong soldier, someone who would be trying to kill me if we were not in a safe zone, or perhaps might kill me that very night. You never knew who was an enemy soldier and who was not. Even the little kids were dangerous: I couldn't allow my jeep to be unprotected, for example, because the Viet Cong had trained children, eight and nine years old, how to booby-trap a jeep. Little kids as young as six years old were taught to sell powerful, pure heroin for 50 cents to American soldiers in an effort to get them hooked on the drug and undermine the morale and discipline within the American fighting force. It was the most ironic cruelty of warfare: You could die just as easily by the hand of a child as you could from the bullet of an adult.

You developed your combat instincts based on that morbid thought. Survival is the purest of instincts heightened by the realities of war, and is not a topic of grand discussion or careful planning. The thing that really got to me was how tenuous security could be in a combat zone. We never announced our plans in advance and never traveled anywhere out and back by the same route. That's how we prevented being ambushed.

I vividly recall a mission in the Binh Thuan Province when the Americans were pulling out. Tiger and I were waiting for Col. Phong's military units to arrive to take over the fire base and convert it to Vietnamese operation, but Tiger's troops were delayed. He said: "That's all right; we can defend it ourselves."

Lieutenant Colonel Woods monitors Tiger's troops as they construct a bridge in Binh Thuan Province, Republic of South Vietnam.

"Just the two of us, Tiger?" I said "This is ridiculous."

"No," he answered, "our two drivers also. One man in each corner."

So deep in VC territory, I retrieved my grenade-launcher from the jeep and lined it up with my .45-caliber pistol and M-16 rifle. There was plenty of ammunition left by the withdrawn U.S. troops. I remember thinking sarcastically, Bullets in abundance—what a relief. Big deal! We covered the area alone for three hours; it seemed an eternity. Col. Phong's support forces finally arrived, and he chewed out the commander for thirty minutes. I called for a helicopter on my radio to evacuate us; my nerves were totally shot.

We couldn't have been in the air more than 50 yards before we were under fire. The startling realization came to us: The VC had been watching us the entire time. Yet why didn't they attack?

"You crazy sonofabitch," I screamed at Tiger, as our helicopter was peppered by rounds of VC fire, bullets penetrating right through the floor. He had that impish grin on his face as our eyes met in the darkness of the chopper. Once again my life had been spared, and I had no idea why. Only years later would I realize the reason. My work on this earth was not done. There was a long-range plan for me.

No doubt Col. Phong was part of that plan—on more than one occasion he saved my life in Vietnam. One day we were on a mission, a multibattalion operation. I was standing on a rice patty dike, which keeps the water in the rice fields. The ground was very dry and covered with crusty old dirt. Tiger was lying down in the ditch beside the dike. He had asked me to obtain Cobra helicopter Gun Ships for a fire mission to support his troops; they had encountered stiff resistance from the VC along the entire front and needed help desperately. The Vietnamese did not have this capability, so American forces had to be used, and I, as his adviser, was the only person who could make the request. As the requested helicopters came on station, I asked Tiger where he wanted the explosives dropped. He said: "Fifty yards in front of my troops."

I said, "Tiger, that's too close."

"OK, how about 75 yards?" he said.

I said, "No, no. How about 100 yards?"

"OK, 100 then," he finally agreed.

I told him to mark the right and left perimeters of his

troops with smoke so that the choppers could locate them, and I gave the heading on which to drop the ordinance. And while I was relaying this information to the gunship commanding officer, I'm vaguely aware that Tiger is hollering at me from the ditch. He's pointing frantically at the ground to my right. I looked around to see nothing but a hunk of fresh dirt.

"Tiger, don't bother me," I yelled. I was focused on monitoring the helicopters and talking to the commander on my radio.

But Tiger was still hollering. This time he was even more agitated as he pointed to the ground to my left side. I noticed a hunk of dirt missing, nothing more.

I told him again, "Look, Tiger, don't bother me anymore!"

After sending the helicopters around for one more pass, I released them, and they returned to base. Then I jumped back down in the ditch with him.

I said, "What the hell were you trying to tell me?"

He said: "You are the coolest adviser I have ever had in my life. A sniper bracketed you. The first shot went to your right. The second shot went to your left. And I expected the third shot to go right through your chest. That's what I was trying to tell you."

But, thankfully, the third shot never came. Why? What happened to the sniper? Why was I so lucky to be spared? I like to think it was so that I could be around to someday raise my own little Tiger.

Immediately after that incident with the sniper, it was my turn to relax, and I turned the fighting over to Tiger. There was a little bamboo thicket nearby, and as I pulled my hat down to shield my eyes from the torrid Asian sun, I snuggled safely in its shade.

I woke up hearing Tiger say: "Woody!"

"What?" I mumbled.

He said, "Don't move."

I didn't.

"There's a bamboo viper about two inches from your right eye," he said quietly. I rolled my eyes to the right to see the wide-open fang-filled mouth and flitting tongue of one of the most venomous snakes in the world, right in front of my face. Have you ever gone eyeball to eyeball with "Mr. No-Shoulders"? I recommend strongly that you don't. I was never so terrified in my life. But I was cool—I had to be, if I was going to live.

Tiger kept telling me, "Don't move."

Second miracle of the day: The viper pulled back into the bamboo. Maybe he decided I was too big to eat, maybe he thought I was a rock. Tiger said, "He's gone." And I set a new world record sprinting out of that bamboo.

Off the battlefield, Tiger Phong and I shared and appreciated our differences and celebrated them, instead of letting them come between us. Establishing close ties with people of different ethnic backgrounds never has been a problem for me. I learned a long time ago how to see into a person's character and measure the trustworthiness, the sincerity. Perhaps that is why it disturbs me so to see the racial segregation and prejudice that is so pervasive in our world today.

I schooled Tiger in the rudiments of jazz music—he really loved Miles Davis—while he taught me a thing or two about Eastern philosophy and religion. He showed me how to eat the cuisine of his culture, and I told stories about the incredible foods I grew up eating and missed so badly. I remember telling him about those big-ass Texas-sized watermelons I had known back in the states, and he thought I was lying. He had never seen a watermelon bigger than a cantaloupe. So I wrote my sister, Freda, who was living in Denver at the time, and asked her to send me some watermelon seeds in a letter. Yes, it was illegal, but what the hell, I was in combat. Tiger and I planted those seeds, and watermelons came up growing like mad. Unfortunately, the gophers got to the watermelons from under the ground, ate the roots, and that was the end of the watermelon experiment. It was a crushing blow to our spirits to find those watermelons destroyed, but Tiger and I had a good laugh about it.

Tiger was only about 5 foot 5 inches tall with a medium build, but he loved to eat—especially my homemade chili. When he would come over to visit, we'd watch movies in the evening and play tennis on the weekends. Those were the kinds of things we shared.

There are a lot of Americans who have the mistaken notion that Vietnamese soldiers weren't any good in combat, that you couldn't trust them. Hell, I trusted Tiger Phong with my life. And vice versa. And he *was* good, very good. I admired his leadership, his tenacity, his absolute fearlessness in combat, sometimes to my chagrin. And the human side of him as well: He was simply a pleasant, compassionate guy. Despite living a soldier's life, all he wanted to do was become a school teacher. He got stuck in a war with no end and no way out. And that is how he ended up—with no way out.

Just last year, I learned that Tiger Phong lived barely a year after the fall of Saigon, dying September 9, 1976, at the age of 47, in the squalor of a Communist "reeducation camp" (an exalted term for a horrifying prison). The cause of death was listed as "heart illness, unable to save," but the sickening truth was that my wartime buddy had been *starved to death*.

I never saw him again after I left Vietnam. I intuitively knew he didn't make it out, and I felt strongly that he would be put into a camp in North Vietnam because of his rank and strong anti-Communist record. The realist in me told me that he couldn't be alive. But the optimist in me said it was possible, although highly improbable. Then you hope and pray anyway. Intellectually, I realized there was very little hope. The spiritual part of me always kept saying: "I hope he made it." I had always envisioned finding him, alive, and reminiscing about some of the things he and I had experienced, things I could never share with anyone else. But that will not happen now. That possibility has been taken away from me.

When I learned that Vietnam had fallen, and that Tiger Phong was likely still there, I vowed that if I ever had another son, I would nickname him Tiger, in the hope that my son would be as strong and courageous as my friend. I had no intentions at that point of having another child—I already had three from my first marriage—but somehow, it helped me feel that I could do something for my friend who had done so much for me. So that is how my son Eldrick came to be known as Tiger Woods. From the time my Tiger was a little boy, I told him stories about the original Tiger. This was my fantasy: that this kid named after Tiger Phong would become famous one day, and my old dear friend would read about a Tiger Woods in the newspaper or see him on television, and he would make the connection and find me. That was the hope that I had harbored all those years. Of course, rationally, I knew that if Tiger Phong had been in a reeducation camp for any length of time, even if he had survived, the chances of him coming out with an unscrambled brain were slim to none. For many years, I had the uneasy feeling that he might be living close by, with a mind so scrambled he would never remember me or hear about his namesake who had, meanwhile, become an international celebrity.

But Tiger Phong, as it turned out, died eight months after Tiger was born.

The complete, devastating story came to light thanks to the efforts of Tom Callahan of *Golf Digest* magazine. Callahan, intrigued by the story behind Tiger's name and the fate of Tiger Phong, gained access to Vietnam by feigning an interest in the growth of golf in that country. Then he defied government censors and began tracking the fate of Lieutenant Colonel Phong. His shocking story, which appeared in the October 1997 issue of *Golf Digest*, detailed the twisted story of his search and the horrifying story of the death of Tiger Phong.

Callahan discovered that after the fall of Saigon, Tiger managed to hide for a while. He even dared to sneak back one last time to see his family—his wife and nine children—before he finally turned himself in and was sent away to a reeducation camp. He survived for about a year, writing letters to his family, before his frail, emaciated body gave out from the hard labor and lack of food. He just keeled over and died. But he didn't quit. Tiger would never quit.

It took ten years for the government to notify his family, who had no idea what had happened to him or even where he was. When they finally learned his fate in 1986, they discovered that he had been buried in a jungle along with other "criminals." His sons found the concrete marker (a miracle in itself, since most of the other markers had been wood, which had rotted away over the years). They unearthed his bones, brought them home, washed each bone by hand and gave their father a proper burial.

The heartbreaking news of Tiger Phong's demise brought the hoping and praying to closure, but it was crushing for me; I cried for a couple of days after I learned that he had died. It was like losing family. My son was my shoulder to cry on, and he was there for me. It makes me so very sad to realize that Tiger Phong is gone from this earth. I couldn't believe that after so many years of waiting, wondering, praying, it was finally over. What a tragic waste, and so unnecessary. I am still tortured by the image of him being starved to death. It hurt when I found out, and it still hurts, even as I write these words.

When the Golf Digest story came to light, so did the shocking discovery that Tiger's widow, Lythi Bich Van, had been living in Tacoma, Washington, since 1994; she was now 61 years old. She had never heard of my Tiger and his golf, nor does she speak much English. But when the magazine arranged for us to meet at my home in southern California, we were instantly connected by our memories of Tiger and our mutual sadness over the events that had finally brought us together.

It was the first time we had ever met, although one of her sons recalled meeting me in Vietnam when his father brought him to my house. I had never visited Tiger at his own house; it was not an accepted practice for American officers to visit the homes of their Vietnamese counterparts during the war. So Tiger always came to my place, which was named "the blue room," after I had it painted infantry blue to honor my branch of the service.

The reunion of our families was bittersweet; it was so painful yet so beautiful. She had two of her children with her. I had Tida, and, of course, my own Tiger. I could instantly see that she was a sweet, pleasant woman; those qualities just stood out, in spite of our language barrier.

It was so important to me that my Tiger witness this incredible encounter, this exchange of emotions, and to feel it, because he is an integral part of this friendship saga. Ironically, it took the crushing news of Tiger Phong's death to bring his story vividly to life for my son. Seeing my emotions, my strong reaction to the news, made him realize what a critical part of my life this had been. He watched me very closely during the visit, concerned about how I was taking it, and how I was holding up under the emotional strain. I only broke down and cried once, when we were talking about Col. Phong being starved to death. I just couldn't handle it.

My son Tiger recalled to our guests: "I never knew him as Tiger Phong. He was Tiger One, the first Tiger."

"It's hard to keep from crying when Earl Woods talks about how much he loved our father," said Tiger Phong's son, Vong Don Phuoc, who translated for his mother as she shared our tears.

I asked her if there was anything I could do for her and her family, but they said there was nothing they needed or wanted. I did give her a copy of my first book, *Training a Tiger,* and inscribed in it: "In honor of Tiger." My Tiger signed the book, as well. I also gave her son one of my Titleist caps with "Earl Woods" monogrammed on it. It was a little bit too big for him, but he didn't care and fell in love with that hat right away.

They gave me, in respect, a picture of Col. Phong, their Tiger. Being with them, looking into their eyes, it really brought me some closure. I told his widow: "Tiger Phong always will be in our hearts. And there always will be a Tiger in my home and in yours." She smiled and nodded. She didn't speak English very well. Yet, somehow, we were speaking the same language.

Out of the clear blue sky, I asked her, "Are you happy?"

Right away, she answered: "Yes." As tears returned to my eyes, I was comforted by that. I know that Tiger's legacy lives on, in our hearts, in our memories and in the very existence of my own son.

Even in light of what happened to Tiger Phong and even considering the controversial social and political ramifications of the Vietnam War, I have no remorse or regret today about my service there. I viewed the experience strictly as a military assignment. I was a military officer assigned to Vietnam. Wartime conditions require a "business as usual" attitude or you cannot survive. So I served my tours, did my duty, and I came home. It was not my job to question policy and procedures. My job was to perform, which I did to the best of my abilities. As a result, I made an easy transition back into the civilian population. I have suffered no aftershocks from time in Vietnam; I have never had any sleepless nights, frightening dreams, weird reactions or flashbacks.

While my military experience reinforced in me the strength that I have, it also showed me that I have the power to make a commitment and keep it. It demonstrated to me that I have the ability and the power to make a difference in people's lives, and I have tried to pass those lessons on to my son.

Chapter Three

· ·

MARRIAGES AND MULLIGANS

I WAS BLESSED as a child to grow up in a family that revolved around the principles of respect and dignity. We took care of each other; we appreciated each other. We knew what it meant to share and care for others.

Today, I am also blessed to have the opportunity to go into communities, into businesses and schools, and talk about these very things. It's a privilege for me to be able to share with others the things I taught to Tiger, the things my mother taught to me.

But it concerns me that people see me as a Mr. Clean, Mr. Do-Good, Mr. Righteous. I am none of these. I don't know any big secrets about life, nor do I profess to. I don't have all the answers. I am not a saint, a genius, a philosopher. I am not an intellectual.

I am only me. I pretend to be nothing else. I have flaws, and faults, just like all of you. Some of them I am not very proud of, but I have learned to handle them. You might not agree with the way I've lived my life, and you may not understand all the choices I've made, but that's fine with me. I try to do my best, and be the best person I know how to be.

When I set out to write this book, it was with the intention of being totally honest, of showing people who I really am, how Tiger became the person he is today and what we stand for. So there are some things about my own life that I feel I should share so that all the pieces of our story fit together. It is important to me that people perceive me accurately, and not as a figment of their imagination.

If you believe nothing else about me, believe this: I am a concerned parent. That is all I can claim to be. I'm no expert on relationships, nor am I a PGA pro. But I have been in this business of parenting for a long time, with two families. Actually, I have had three families, counting my childhood, where I was on the receiving end of my mother's terrific parenting skills.

Yet somehow, I turned that good experience into a license to start out on my own thinking I knew everything and needed no advice or help with my next family.

You might look at my life today and see it as trouble-free, charmed. But let me assure you, that was not the case some 30 years ago, when my first marriage deteriorated and ended in divorce.

The dissolution of a marriage seldom involves one particular incident or the shortcomings of one individual. It entails a combination of a couple's misdeeds, miscalculations and unfortunate circumstances. In the case of my first marriage, I'm sure I contributed my share to its failure. In retrospect, it was not a very solid relationship from the beginning. There were too many issues, flawed circumstances, factors you overlook when that love bug first hits you early in life. I married too young. I was inexperienced, and the marriage didn't turn out as I expected. I am quite sure she has her side of the story.

The first mistake I made was in the selection of a mate. I went against the advice of my older sisters who vehemently rejected the idea of my first wife, but Mr. Know-It-All prevailed. And so, with no notification to my family, I got married the day before I was to enter the military service as a 2nd lieutenant. It came as a staggering shock to everyone, but Mr. Wiseguy knew that he wouldn't be around to have to listen to their flak, because he was going into the service.

Armed with this infinite wisdom, poor selection, no experience and a cocky attitude, I was doomed for failure. And fail I did.

At that time, servicemen spent little time with their families because of commitments and assignments to which the families were not authorized to be brought. In my case, as a young 2nd lieutenant, I finished school and was immediately assigned to Germany. I was not authorized to bring my wife, because there was no government housing available. But I thought I knew it all, so I went ahead and sent for her anyway and decided we would live in the German economy among the civilian population, until government quarters became available.

What a mistake: I'll never forget the commotion my wife and I caused as we walked through the streets of Pirmasens, shopping for our new apartment. We stopped traffic, caused traffic jams. I couldn't understand it and finally asked my landlord, "What is the problem?"

He looked at me, clearly embarrassed, and said, "They are looking for your tails."

"Tails? What tails?" I asked, completely baffled. And he explained: During World War II, the white soldiers told the Germans that black soldiers had tails. That's what everyone was looking for. Obviously, I was one of the first black soldiers that they had seen, and my wife was clearly the first black female they had seen. That was my introduction to Germany. Boy, do we export our prejudices. We utilize our movies, our books, our magazines, all to perpetuate our insecurities and biases to foster this "Step'n'fetchit" image of blacks in the U.S. Young black military personnel have had to pay for this over decades, and it should stop.

No doubt, the positive outcome of my first marriage was

the birth of our three children. My eldest son is Earl Jr., also known as "Den," short for his middle name Dennison, same as mine. That is how the family made a distinction between the two of us. Next is my son Kevin Dale, and then my daughter Royce Renay. Two boys and a girl.

It was not a very happy situation for any of us, primarily because I was miserable in the relationship and I was away from home for very long stretches of time (at this point, my wife and children were living in California). I tried to make it as good an environment as I could for the children—when I was there. But while I was in the service, I would be gone on assignment for a year or longer; it is unfortunate, but I was never there on a consistent basis.

When people ask me, "How long were you married the

After a delightful summer in New York, I'm on my way to Vietnam. The kids stayed with us all summer. L-R: Earl, Tida, Royce, Kevin, Den.

At the end of my first tour of duty in Vietnam, my return home had been delayed because policy dictated that you did not leave until your replacement was fully trained and ready to function. I was being replaced by four men, and by the time they were competent and ready, it was more than a month after my family had expected me home; they had no idea when I might show up.

I arrived back in California in the middle of the night and knocked on the door. After a while, I heard someone inside.

"Who's there?" Barbara said.

"It's me," I answered.

Long pause. "Who is me?" came the voice from inside the house.

"Open up the damn door," I demanded.

Then, finally recognizing who it was, Barbara said: "Oh, okay."

My daughter, Royce, who was just a little girl, came stumbling out of her bedroom. She looked up and said: "Mommy, who is that man?" (What a wonderful reception after an extended tour in Vietnam, right?)

That's when it really hit me: *Lord, my daughter doesn't even recognize me. And she has grown into a completely different person than she was before I left.* I had become a stranger in my own house. Or so I thought. Thank goodness, the next morning my daughter was bouncing on my knee. She had finally placed me in her young mind.

All of these things made me appreciate years later how important it was to be there for Tiger's entire developmental life. I appreciated the opportunity to be on the scene with him, watching him go through all the phases children go through. I was able to help guide his progression, his growth, on a consistent, daily basis. I was there for Tiger, all the time. I had missed out on that quality time interaction with my other children, and I vowed never to make that mistake again.

By the time I returned from my second tour of duty in

first time?" I always say, "Too long." Looking back
marriage was a tragic mistake, despite the factors that
me to Barbara in the first place, and I knew early into
riage that it was headed for trouble. But after Den wa
felt a strong obligation to stay in the marriage so that
would have a complete family, mother and father. I wa
ing of my child's welfare, not my own. I think that
responsibility of any parent. Well, the first child was fol
by another and yet another, and even when it became clea
the marriage was not working, I was deeply committed t
children. So I hung on as long as I could; I felt I did the b
could under the circumstances. Years later, when we finally
divorced, I told my kids that I had hung on so long so th
could be there for them. When I told them about the divo
they said, "Daddy, what took so long?" They knew. Tha
when I learned: You can't fool children. They know wha
going on. They know you and they know what is working an
what is not.

If I have any regret, it is that my time in the service forced
me to be away from them. No question, the kids suffered from
my long absences, and I admit that I am to blame for that. I
would come back from an overseas assignment and realize I
had three completely different children; they had evolved into
new phases of their development. That was my own problem
to deal with, not theirs. Their problem was that they badly
needed the stabilizing force of a father. They did not have that
while I was away.

One time I came home from overseas and discovered that
my son Kevin, who had been a natural left-handed hitter, had
suddenly become a right-handed batter. When I asked him
why he had switched, Kevin said: "Well, everybody else is
right-handed." It made such an impression on me, knowing
that this never would have happened if I had been home. My
son had needed guidance in this and other things, and I wasn't
home to offer it.

Vietnam, I saw that divorce was inevitable. My only concern at that point was my children. California law says you own half of your property following a divorce, but I gave almost everything I had for the house in San Jose. I did that for the kids. I promised the kids that when I retired from military service, I would move back to California to be near them. They were living in San Jose in the family home I gave to Barbara. I didn't want to uproot them in any way; the reason I bought that house in the first place was so they wouldn't become military vagabonds, dragging after their father all over the world. I wanted them to always have a home.

So I gave her all the furniture. We had a new car and an old car; I gave her the new station wagon. I supported the kids completely and told them that when they turned 18, they could come live with me. That was when I knew that my fears of losing them were unfounded: Just like clockwork, when Den got to be 18, he came to me. When Kevin turned 18, he came, too. When Royce became 18, she moved in with me.

They each lived with me until they were 21, and I put them through what I call "Woods' Finishing School." It was an effort on my part to make up for lost time, lost opportunities. We had a wonderful time together, and when they each turned 21, they headed out into the cruel hard world on their own, with my help, of course. And I assure you, parents, the help is still coming.

I did the best I could, and they knew it, although you can only do so much with young adults. We have been close ever since. Unfortunately, you just can't make up for everything that you were supposed to do, especially during the formative and developmental years. But they are now and forever my kids, even though they are in their 40s.

That is one of the biggest lessons I've learned about parenting—it never ends. You may think your responsibilities will end when your children are grown and have children of their own, but they don't look at it that way. So today, I still find myself closely involved with my grown children, and I see no end.

For the record: I am aware of the spiteful, unfounded innuendo from certain factions of the media that I somehow abandoned these children in favor of their younger brother Tiger. It bothers me greatly to think that my own children—who all think of Tiger as their youngest brother—have been pursued by reporters and pressed for details about their personal relationships with Tiger and me. I am the first to admit that while my first three children were growing up, I was a much different parent (and person) than I was years later to Tiger: I was much older and wiser by the time Tiger was born, and far more involved as a father since I was no longer in the military. But there has never been a time in their lives—throughout their childhood, during the difficult years while I was away in Vietnam, after my divorce from their mother—that I didn't put their welfare first, and they know that. Right now, two of them live near me; Royce lives in San Jose, and Kevin lives in nearby Milpitas, California. Den since has moved to Phoenix, Arizona, but we all remain close. I also have three adorable grandchildren, including one little one who just might follow in her Uncle Tiger's golf shoes.

The final chapter to my first marriage was written in 1996 when, after having been divorced for almost 30 years, Barbara took me to court. She had remarried following our divorce, and her husband subsequently died. And, all of a sudden, out of the clear blue sky, she took me to court. Papers were served on me. She was suing me for 50 percent of my retirement pay, retroactive to when I first retired, with interest. She also wanted 50 percent of my retirement pay from that day until I die. Thirty years after the divorce! Even the kids told her: "What are you doing? This is totally ridiculous." But she was adamant and continued her legal course of action. Of course, the law is very specific. Among other things, she had remarried, and I no longer had any responsibility for her welfare. The case was thrown out of court.

The next great golfer in the Woods family, my seven-year-old granddaughter Cheyenne, lives in Phoenix, Arizona, and has made steady development.

As with so many things in my life, I feel now that my first marriage was a test. The Lord said: "Let's give this guy a boy, and see how he handles it. Give him another one. Well, let's give him a girl and see how he handles that." Then He put me through the trials and tribulations of an unhappy marriage. He was testing me, always testing me and preparing me. By the time I was in a position to remarry, I was better prepared to handle children. And that's what He had in mind. I can see it all clearly now.

It was some three decades ago, while my first marriage was falling apart, that I was thousands of miles away on military assignment in Thailand, completely unaware of the life-altering experience that was about to present itself to me.

I look at that time in my life as a path that came to a fork. The road divided, and I had to choose which path to follow. This is my theory about life: It is a road with many forks. Make your choice, and never look back to second-guess yourself. The irrevocable fact of life is that there is always going to be yet another fork which will require yet another decision. Make the best of your choice, accept responsibility for it, and be prepared for the next fork.

As a result of striking out in my first marriage, I was a lot more prudent in selecting a second mate. Similar to every bump in the road I have encountered over the years, this setback in my personal life inspired me to try to turn a negative ordeal into something positive, regardless of how hurtful and arduous that disappointment was at the time. To me, "playing through" is the ultimate manifestation of a positive attitude; it's the belief that you *can* overcome, that you *can* keep going. Anyone who has been through a divorce knows the emotional turmoil of wondering if he or she could ever go through it all again. Playing through is rarely the course of least resistance.

When you play casual golf among friends, if you shank a ball off the tee on your first attempt, it is called a Mulligan, and in friendly company, you are allowed to pick up your ball and give it another shot. I suppose my first marriage was a Mulligan of sorts, because I was given another shot at marriage. It really changed my life forever. I am convinced that meeting my current wife, the former Kultida Punswad, was yet another predetermined event.

It was quite hilarious how we first met, really. I was a special services officer in Thailand, and my military assignment that day involved hiring approximately 4,000 people from around the whole country for various recreation sites. On this particular day, I was heading over to meet with the civilian personnel officer, along with my assistant, who happened to be white.

Kultida, whom I always call Tida (pronounced Tee-da), was the office receptionist. As we approached, she automatically deferred to the white guy—my assistant. She looked up at him and said: "May I help you?"

Tida enjoys a ride on the beach in Thailand.

My assistant said that we were there to speak to the personnel officer, that we had an appointment to meet with him.

"What is your name?" she asked.

He told her: "Colonel Woods."

He meant me, of course, but she didn't get it.

Tida went into the personnel officer's office to check on his availability and came back. "OK, he will see you right now," she said. She escorted us into his office and returned to her desk.

Shortly after we began the meeting, I pulled my assistant aside and said, "Hey, you handle the details. I'm going out to talk to the receptionist."

And that's what I did. I was so drawn to the striking woman with the expressive eyes. I approached her and, boy, did she blush. She had figured out by then that *I* was the colonel, not the assistant: She had seen me through the huge picture window with my feet up on the desk, and she realized she had made a terrible mistake. As she started to apologize, I said: "No, no. Don't worry about it." That seemed to make it easier for us to talk on a more personal level.

We chatted, made small talk, and she laughed easily. Her face was aglow and her eyes sparkled. I immediately felt a bond with her. Finally, I got her to agree to a date with me at 9 o'clock.

My assistant finally came out of the meeting and said, "Sir, are you ready to go?" By this time, I was practically oblivious to the original purpose of our office visit. I looked up, startled, and said, "Yep, I'm all set." Boy, was I ever!

I could hardly wait for night to arrive.

At 9 o'clock that night, I was waiting at our agreed-upon meeting spot. And I sat there. . . . 15 minutes, 20 minutes, 30 minutes elapsed. But she didn't show. Finally, I said to myself, "Oh, well, I guess I've been stood up." I felt deflated and darned disappointed. With head bowed, I returned to my quarters completely depressed.

The next morning was a Thai holiday, but we Americans had to work anyway. My office was located on the seventh floor of an imposing building with a restaurant on the first floor, where the American military personnel would usually go during breaks and meals, so the restaurant employees knew us all very well. Well, I had barely arrived at the office when I got a call from the restaurant manager, telling me that two ladies were waiting for me there. I couldn't imagine who it could be, so I went down to see what the heck was going on. Sure enough, it was Tida and her friend, the chaperone.

Tida was irate. She began ranting and raving: "It is past 9 o' clock and you were not there!"

I stood there, dumbfounded, until I could finally say, "Look, where were you last night?"

She said, "What do you mean last night?"

And then it hit me. She thought I had meant 9 o'clock in the morning. It never occurred to her that a 9 o'clock date might be at night; she went to bed by 9 o'clock every night.

After I explained to her the miscommunication, we both had a good laugh.

I went back upstairs to the office, told my colleagues about the misunderstanding, and Tida and I spent the day going to two or three Buddhist Wats (a Wat is a temple). We went to see the reclining Buddha, did some sightseeing, had a wonderful dinner, and enjoyed easy conversation. Our entire first date was spent in church, since it was a religious holiday and every native of Thailand was in church. She had thought that was what I wanted to do—take her to church. No wonder she agreed so easily. And I had thought it was my charm and good looks.

I immediately liked her presence, her poise, her confidence. She had a very engaging personality and was very outgoing. And she was a stunningly attractive woman. There was nothing lacking about her. Her English was very good, too. I was drawn to her immediately. Who wouldn't have been?

It was not normal for a Thai woman of class such as Tida to associate with American soldiers. It just didn't happen in Thailand. But Tida was different. Very earnest and sincere, yet daring and willing to go against cultural tradition to pursue her dreams and aspirations.

Like me, Tida comes from a very mixed multiethnic heritage. Her grandfather on her mother's side was white, and her grandfather on her father's side was Chinese. Her uncle still lives in mainland China. Her mother's mother is a native Thai. And her father is Thai. I, on the other hand, am part American Indian (Shawnee), Chinese, Caucasian and African-American.

No wonder we consider our Tiger a universal kid. We've got Africa, Asia, Europe, and America covered.

I know without doubt now that it was preordained for us to meet. Tida just happened to be working at the right place at the right time for me to see and meet her. There was some force that brought us together, and He delivered the message to me straight, right from the start: "Go to church! You don't take her to nightclubs. You take her to a church." That set the tone for my relationship with Tida. It was based on respect.

I returned home to the States after my tour of duty in Thailand, but Tida had my heart. Subsequently, Barbara and I would get a divorce, and a year later, Tida would come to America to become my wife.

Tida agrees it was fate that brought us together and enticed her to leave her native country to come to America, despite considerable resistance from her family. Until she met me in her mid-20s, she had grown up and lived her whole life in the Bangkok area. It was a courageous decision on her part. In Thailand, if you are a native of that country and you marry a foreigner, you lose the right to own property in Thailand, a stipulation designed to prevent foreigners from coming in and taking ownership. No question, the Thai people tended to look at foreigners with major reservations.

If that hurdle wasn't enough, the age-old problem of racial prejudice popped its ugly head into the picture. Any foreigner was bad news, but a black military man was even worse. In other words, there did not appear to be any decent future in being associated with an American black soldier.

So Tida had to face that stigma. But she trusted me, and

eventually came to the United States against the will of her mother and most of her family. It took a lot of guts and faith in me for her to do that. And she was greatly ostracized by some of her people for her decision. But she certainly got her revenge: When she returned to Thailand many years later as the mother of Tiger Woods, she was suddenly transformed into a heroine. Tida reunited with her many relatives—three brothers, a sister, nieces, nephews, aunts and uncles. Nearly 1,000 well-wishers greeted Tiger at the airport when he arrived for a tournament at the Thai Country Club (which he won by 10 strokes), and the entire country—including heads of state—turned inside out to make them feel welcome and comfortable. How quickly fame and fortune affect the attitudes of people.

I returned from overseas in 1973 and lived in New York for a while, where Tida joined me and we were married.

After I retired from the service, I moved to California, where prejudice found us once again, particularly in our efforts

I proudly marched in the 1973 Memorial Day Parade in New York City while stationed at Fort Hamilton, Brooklyn, New York.

Yes, Tida was there also.

to purchase a home. I had told my kids that I would return to San Jose to be near them; they still lived with their mother in the house I had bought for them. I learned that the parents of my second son's girlfriend were divorcing and wanted to sell their custom-built home in San Jose, so I pursued the possibility of buying it. I went so far as to negotiate a price before leaving New York. When Tida saw it, she was thrilled; we were coming from a tiny New York apartment. This house had walk-in closets, a fireplace in the upstairs bedroom, an oversized master bedroom, his and her closets. It was gorgeous. And I was in a position to buy.

Well, we liked it so much that the price of the house suddenly went up by $5,000 overnight. Coincidence? I doubt it. And they were black, too. So I said no thanks. I asked my kids what they thought about my moving to southern California, only about a 50-minute plane ride from where they lived. No problem, they said. So I came down to southern California and started house-hunting in Los Alamitos. But every house we liked was suddenly off the market. Not for sale, as soon as it was discovered that we were non-white. This happened four times. The fifth time, we went into a house being sold by a real estate agent who personally owned it. As soon as I walked in, the guy said, "No co-op."

My broker said to me, "Come on, let's go."

As we drove away I asked, "What did he mean by that?"

He said, "That's real estate slang for 'We will not sell this house to your client under any circumstances.'"

He added, "You don't need this." As it turned out, he owned a condominium in Los Alamitos, which he was willing to rent to us on a temporary basis. We checked it out, liked it, and agreed to stay there for a year before buying a house. And that is what we did. I rented my broker's personal condominium for a year.

We even encountered problems with discrimination there. Tida would be in the swimming pool at the complex, where all the other ladies would go to socialize. But when I would come out to the pool and hug my wife, everyone would scatter. Suddenly stony silence would descend as they would get out of the water and leave. We knew we weren't welcome.

When my oldest son, Earl Jr., turned 18 and decided to begin living with us, he was harassed by the Los Alamitos police while parking my 1965 Mustang in my garage. The police drove up and slammed on their brakes. As my son got out of the car, they slammed him up against the wall, made him spread-eagle, and they patted him down.

"What are you doing here?" one policeman asked.

"I live here," my son answered, scared out of his mind.

"You live here with who?" the policeman demanded.

"My father," Earl Jr. answered.

"Where?" they asked.

"Right here. This is my garage," he stammered.

And the policeman said: "Well, we're not accustomed to seeing people like you in this neighborhood."

This was 1975! But I had taught my sons to never be flippant with police authority, just get their badge numbers. Earl Jr. got both numbers and told me about the incident. I just happened to be in a bowling league in which the police department had a team. These guys all knew me, so I took the two numbers and told my friends what had happened, how he had been harassed, and asked them would they take care of the problem. They said, "Just leave it to us." We never had any additional problems after that. It didn't make up for the incident, but it felt like a little bit of progress.

Tida was not surprised at the extent of racism in America when she came to the United States. When she arrived, I gave her some very up-front advice. I said: "I know you are from Thailand. I know you are Thai. But in the United States, there are only two colors—white and non-white. Whites will let you know without a doubt that you are non-white; you'll see it in their actions and reactions to you. So don't think that you can ever be a full-fledged citizen here in the United States."

She quickly found this to be the case. It was not a shock to her; it was merely a validation of what I had said, which somehow made her transition to America a lot easier. She, too, was learning the meaning of "playing through."

After our marriage, I was in no rush to start another family. At first, I was more concerned with retirement then, getting myself reestablished in civilian life. I had just completed 20 years of service, and I needed to figure out what to do next. I wanted to go in a completely different direction, try something new. I felt I had something very important to do with my life, something very important. I had no idea I would find it in a little guy named Tiger.

Having more children had never been in my plans: I was already in my 40s, with three children. But Tida felt differently—in Thai culture, a marriage is not recognized as fully consummated unless children are born from that union. I was

Tida plays with Toti at our New York apartment. This is her first dog and the love of her life.

almost 44 when this little bundle of energy named Eldrick Woods came bursting into our lives in 1975. And what a joy he was.

Tida took to motherhood like a duck to water, and she generally does not receive enough credit for the rearing of Tiger. I believe the groundwork for a child comes from the mother, because she spends so much time with the youngster in the formative years. In so many respects, Tiger was raised as an Asian child, not as an American. The way Tiger was taught to respect his parents and other adults, to rely on his instincts and feelings, to be unselfish and generous . . . these are all tenets of Asian philosophy and culture that he has embraced. We never hired a baby-sitter for Tiger as a child; Tida always felt that he

*A dapper Earl enjoys a
moment of jazz music at
the pad in New York.*

was much more important than attending any social event. She
believed that parenting was a 24-hour job, not just two or three
hours. And she was right.

By the time we discovered that the little guy had an affin-
ity for golf, Tida and I made a personal commitment to each
other that we would devote all of our energies and finances to
assure that he had the best that we could give him. Total commitment! Well, something had to give, and it was our relationship. The priority became Tiger, and not each other, And in retrospect I see that our relationship began to decline from that
day on. Not the trust, not the respect, just that unbridled love.
You see, my favorite expression is, "Love is a given, trust and
respect are earned." And we had ample opportunities to
develop great trust and respect for each other. And that still
prevails today. If I had it to do over again, I would do the same

thing, because it meant that I was able to spend all of the time with Tiger, and be there for him on a day-by-day basis, assist in his development, guide his growth and maturity and, more than anything, be his friend.

The outgrowth of this, and I allude to my previous comment that you can't fool the kids, is that Tiger was aware of the situation between his parents. Even when he was young, during our trips around the nation to golf tournaments, we had in-depth conversations about relationships, my specific relationship with his mother, his future relationships, etc. From these discussions came his pledge that "when I become a professional golfer, Dad, I will take care of Mom." He instinctively knew that one day he would be in a situation to do that, and it was something he really wanted to do. I might also add that this is a Thai cultural tradition.

And so when he did in fact become a pro, his first order of business was to buy his mother her dream home in Tustin, California. Tida had always wanted a large showy home, while I preferred our small intimate home in nearby Cypress. I chose to remain in the family home where Tiger was raised, so I could be in touch with the childhood memories of him while I was writing not only this book but my first book, *Training a Tiger*, as well. Who knows, maybe one day Tiger's childhood home will become a national monument!

What happened to our marriage? Not much really. I have a belief that relationships never end; they just change their form. If your father dies, that relationship doesn't end; it just changes. The same has occurred in my relationship with Tida. It hasn't ended, and never will. Today, we're best friends, have a beautiful amicable relationship and ardently follow Tiger's development and progress every step of the way, still fully supportive. She has her home, I have mine. Some people would call that separated. I call it affluence. The thing that still remains strong to this day is trust and respect. And that will never change.

PART 2

· ·

ALONG CAME A TIGER

● ●

Chapter Four

RAISING A GOOD KID (WHO HAPPENS TO LOVE GOLF)

T IGER WAS ACTIVE from tee to green, even before he was born.

When Tida was seven months pregnant with Tiger, I was invited to play in a golf tournament at Lake Shastina in northern California. We drove there, and Tida walked the golf course with me. Tiger would be very active inside Tida's stomach— kicking and moving around—until she approached the area around the green. Then, whenever a golf ball hit the green, it reverberated against the volcanic surface and produced a thumping sound, similar to a drum. Tiger apparently reacted to the vibrations. He would suddenly be very still and quiet. But as soon as we moved onto the next hole, Tiger would start kicking and stirring again. And as soon as we got to the green, he was quiet as a mouse. It was the most bizarre occurrence. He seemed to know golf protocol while he was still in the womb.

I was not witness to the births of my three older children because of my military obligations. So I was excited to actually see the birth of Tiger. I went through the prenatal training classes with Tida, determined to be there to watch and appreciate this blessed event.

On the day Tiger was born, Dec. 30, 1975, Tida began experiencing labor pains and we went to the hospital. After several hours, I told her: "Hey, you are going to have to knock this off and get going, because today is Dec. 30, and I need that tax deduction."

Even though she was in pain, Tida had the good humor to laugh. She was doing all of the work, and I was trying to provide a little comic relief. But I quickly learned that it was not the moment for comedy.

Tiger was born that evening. As I watched my son come into the world, I suppose my combat experience came in handy: I didn't get sick watching the graphic delivery, I didn't become nauseated, I didn't get overwhelmed. I simply observed. Of course, I had the easy part.

When I first saw Tiger, he was purple. I remember joking, to no one in particular: "God, he is ugly!" I watched the doctor and nurses clean him, getting him ready to meet his exhilarated but exhausted mother. I couldn't get over the reality of how ugly a newborn baby was. But it was good news all around: Tiger was healthy, and Tida was fine, too. I felt comforted, reassured and awfully proud. And I had my tax exemption!

Believe me, I had not the slightest lofty aspiration for Tiger when he was first born; I certainly wasn't pondering how to turn this wonderful creature into an international superstar. Heck, we didn't even know in advance whether the baby was going to be a boy or a girl. We just hoped that the baby would be healthy. Other than that, I intuitively knew that his destiny would be shaped by a much greater power than his parents.

I knew how important it was for my wife to have a baby. It was Tida's first child. I already had three, so to me it wasn't the all-consuming event that it was to her, at the time. But once we made the decision to have a child together, I made the commitment to be there at home with Tiger. My older children had

At two months, Tiger learns to balance on Earl's hand. He later learned to stand.

missed out on having their father around while I was in the service, and I lost the opportunity to watch them grow up and fully contribute to their young lives. I would not repeat that situation.

When we came home with our newborn, I put Tiger in his crib, and I turned on jazz; I wanted jazz to be his first musical experience. I would sit by his crib, watch him sleep and listen to jazz . . . those are moments I will never forget. It was the start of our private time together.

So at a very early age, we shared a love for music. But we were about to share something else that would change our lives—as well as the lives of many others—for all time.

I was 42 years old when I took up the game of golf, just a year or so before Tiger was born, and like so many golfers (and you know who you are), I worked hard on my swing, constantly trying to improve. I even set up a net in the garage, so I could practice at home and at night. So when Tiger was six months old, barely old enough to sit, I would set his high chair up in the garage as I practiced my swing, hitting into that net. From the very start, he was fascinated—he had an incredible attention span of almost two hours, and he never took his eyes off me.

Always a professional sleeper, Tiger gets in some practice "Z" time on Dad's stomach, his favorite resting place.

I'm mobile now. Yeah for the walker! Tiger at four months.

For those who have accused me of force-feeding Tiger a nonstop diet of golf instruction, let me set the record straight. I never had any intention of teaching Tiger anything about the rudiments of golf. I didn't put him in the garage with me so that he could learn to play; I brought him with me for the company so that we could be together. The discovery that he could hit the hell out of the ball was as stunning to me as it was to everyone else, and I take no credit for his natural ability. He must have been learning through some sort of mystical osmosis (although I did have a pretty good swing to copy).

This is my pool. Care to join me? Tiger at 18 months.

No fear—Tiger at 21 months.

No one would believe it today, but as Tiger grew, there were indeed days that he would take two shots and he wouldn't be up to my drive yet. Of course, he was only four years old at the time, but I love to remind him of those days anyway. We parents have pride also.

His big deal back then was to say, "Someday, Daddy, I am going to be able to hit my drive up to your drive in two shots."

Then it was: "One day, Daddy, I want to hit the ball as long as you."

Finally, he began to realize he was going to eventually be able to hit the ball farther than me. Then I started hearing: "You know, Daddy, I am getting longer and longer. And you're getting shorter and shorter."

Very funny.

From the very early years of his life, Tiger could always hit the golf ball a long way. He was not only long with all his clubs, he was also very accurate. I taught him to play the game from the green back to the tee; in other words, I told him the driver would be the last club in his bag that he would master. So he was not hitting the ball inordinately long with his driver when he was nine or ten years old, when he had this great growth spurt. And suddenly he was getting distance out of that driver that could only be described as extraordinary. From then on, it was just kiss it good-bye. It was just a matter of time—for me.

Tiger realized at an early age that he was good at golf. Unlike other sports, you can tell at a pretty early age whether you have the ability to be a good golfer, mainly because you don't have to measure up to teammates, and your individual skills can be more easily identified. In baseball, you might be able to hit a fastball or curve at one level, but not at a higher level when the pitching gets tougher. In basketball, you can be

I love you, Pooh!

out there shooting baskets by yourself and hit them all, but you might be the slowest guy on the block and never keep up with anybody on the other team. In football, you may not be the right size. But in golf, it's you and the ball. You know, sometimes at a very early age.

At the age of two Tiger already was analyzing the swings of grown men. "Look, Daddy," Tiger would say. "That man has a reverse pivot!" By the age of three, he was beating ten-year-old boys. When he was five, he was signing autographs. Actually, he was printing autographs in block letters, because he did not know how to write in script yet.

By the age of six, Tiger already had made a hole-in-one. Actually, two of them.

When he was real small, people would ask him, "How did you get so good, Tiger?"

And he would answer: "Practice, practice, practice, *ooooh*." The "ooooh" must have come from something he heard on TV.

But the real point was that he already understood what it took to be successful. The first thing I taught Tiger, aside from the love of the game of golf, was the love of practice. That prevails in him today—the sheer joy of practicing, of having fun while practicing. I taught him that there are no shortcuts. Nobody owes you anything. The game doesn't owe you anything. You get out of it what you put into it.

So he has never expected an easy road to success. He recognizes that hard work, somehow or another, brings about good results, and is an integral part of the process.

By the time he was six years old, a first-grader, Tiger was asking us to purchase golf video tapes. I even got some special audio tapes with subliminal messages. He would take the written key messages from the tape and tack them to the wooden bookshelf in his bedroom. He'd turn on this tape while practicing his swing, and he'd also watch videos of old Masters golf tournaments. We indulged him because it was a legitimate pur-

Toba and Tiger take a break from the tough world of football (2 years, 11 months).

suit, and Tiger was enjoying early success. Give him credit: He was dogged in his pursuit of excellence.

To say the least, he continued to improve his game.

Because of Tiger's tremendous love of golf, Tida and I used that as a platform for discipline. She set the rules at home, and the first rule she established with Tiger was that he had to do his homework before he could play golf. Tiger, you have to understand, was not a normal child intellectually; he had a tremendous capacity for learning things beyond his years. Don't attribute it to me; it must have been a fringe benefit. When he was only three years old, his mom wrote out a multiplication table for him. Tiger would go through that multiplication table over and over and over again. Every day. And he learned it. He also learned how to add and subtract and divide. In school, math was his favorite subject, and that is directly attributed to Tida's early training.

But even before he knew the multiplication table, and before he learned how to add in school, Tiger knew what a par

Riding is riding as Tiger pretends to be a cowboy at three-and-a-half years.

Christmas, birthday, what difference does it make? It's about presents!

Tiger celebrates his new dirt bike. He gives his old tricycle to his half-brother Den.

Tiger at three enjoys the Disney characters at Disneyland, Anaheim, California.

4 hole was, and he knew what par 5 was. He could just look at them and tell. Before he could count to 10, he could tell you if you had a double bogey on a par 5. He also could tell you if you had a birdie on a par 5. How he did this, I have no idea. But Tiger was keeping his score and everybody else's score at the same time. And he'd let you know, too. There was no chance to pad your score when Tiger was around.

Tida played a tremendous role in Tiger's early development. She was his close companion and tutor, and during the week she was the one who took him to all of the golf tournaments as a young child while I was at work. She was the one who kept score for each group he played in. She was the unofficial cheerleader, the den mother. And Tida would root for all

Tiger at four demonstrates his strength by lovingly lifting his monster puppy Boom Boom.

of the kids, so Tiger had to learn that it was okay for mom to root for the other kids, too. He was learning early to share.

By the time Tiger was five, word of this child prodigy began to circulate, and suddenly he was being asked to appear on local and national television. People had to see for themselves that there was this tiny guy who could golf as well as a grown man—if not better—and so Tiger made appearances on *That's Incredible* and *Eye on L.A.* and *The Mike Douglas Show,* as well as many others.

So at an early age, he learned to deal with large doses of attention, the type of scrutiny that understandably makes most children crawl into their shells. But Tiger seemed to thrive on

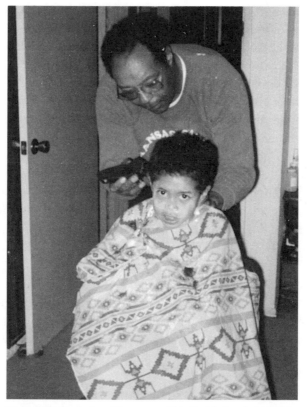

Hold still! Dad gives Tiger one of his first haircuts in 1980.

the spotlight. He wouldn't showboat, but he would somehow improve his performance level. I noticed years ago that whenever there was a television camera on him, or if he came into the final hole of a tournament where there was a crowd around the green, Tiger always performed better. And he would often execute miracle shots.

I felt it was very important that Tiger be well-schooled on how to act in public. Remember my mother's admonitions to me about Joe Louis? "Don't you dare talk the way Joe Louis talks when you grow up," she admonished me. "You learn to speak properly." No question, I instinctively recalled that warning as I watched my own son make his first media appearances. I finally understood why she had been so adamant: If the whole world is watching, you'd better look good, speak good, and be good! So it was very important to me that he was articulate in front of the media.

It was equally important that he never developed an "attitude," never conveyed the slightest impression that he thought he was better than anyone else. We were able to keep him humble. As much as we loved Tiger, we never spoiled him. I remember Tiger as a child watching John McEnroe act up during a tennis match, throwing a temper tantrum on national television. There was a right and wrong way to behave, we said, and Tiger would have to learn the good from the bad. Can you imagine the impact of a black McEnroe-type becoming the first minority superstar in golf? God, how awful that would have been.

One of the biggest shocks Tiger had early on was the realization that some kids cheated at golf. He just couldn't get over that. He was four years old and he came home from a tournament that his mom had taken him to. He said, "Daddy, those kids cheat," and he was astute enough to describe how they did it. The kid was smart.

He said, "This kid was in the sand trap and he touched the sand behind the ball and he didn't count a stroke."

Tiger at three and a half receives his first championship trophy as winner of a pitch, putt and drive contest at Navy Golf Course in Cypress, California.

Tiger and I take a playful break during tournament competition.

Tiger plays a match with CBS Sports commentator Jim Hill.

I asked Tiger if he would ever do that. He said, "No."

So the lesson that day was: "Just because other people cheat doesn't mean you have to cheat. You play the game by the rules and play it fair."

A lot of the same things I have taught Tiger were things I learned from my parents. I upgraded and modernized them, but fundamentally they were the same points, perspectives and lessons I was taught as a child. It is more important to be a good person than to be a great golfer. That all comes from my parents—my mother particularly.

Tiger was five years old when he appeared on the television program *That's Incredible,* which was taped in downtown Los Angeles. There was a little girl on the program, about 11 years old, who had amazing abilities as a weight lifter; she was able to lift hosts John Davidson, Fran Tarkenton and Cathy Lee Crosby on a special harness they had rigged up.

I looked at Tiger and asked, "Can you do that?"

Tiger said, "No, Daddy."

I said, "Well, she is a special person. She is special in weightlifting. You are special in golf. And there are a lot of special people in the world in whatever they do. You are one of them. Do you understand that?"

Tiger said, "Yes, Daddy."

And I broke out into goose bumps, because I realized he really did understand.

I wanted to do my part to cultivate and refine the amazing skills I was witnessing in my son at such an unbelievably young age. By the time Tiger was seven, I realized it was time for me to make sure his mental game was progressing as rapidly as his physical game. So I put him through "Woods' Finishing School."

I would try to distract Tiger on the golf course by jingling the change in my pocket before he attempted a putt, or I would pump the brake on the golf cart before his backswing on an iron shot. It was psychological warfare—I did everything with the best intentions, of course. I wanted to make sure he would never run into anybody who was tougher mentally than he was, and we achieved that. Eventually, nothing I did to distract him during practice rounds could make the boy flinch or falter. He developed nerves of steel. One time a security marshal's walkie-talkie accidentally kicked on at top volume while Tiger was in the middle of his backswing. Tiger later said he never heard it.

One of the biggest arguments Tiger and I ever had was when I changed his par from a 7 to a 6. You see, I created this establishment of his par to keep the game fun, interesting and competitive for him. We were playing together, and I said: "You can get there to the green now in four strokes. So your par is six."

Tiger at four learns to chip in the family garage with his Dad.

He was furious. "Oh, no, Daddy. No, no, no," he fought. Then he would proceed to birdie the damn thing anyway.

I tried to prepare him as best I could to win. That was the goal. After a tournament, we would talk over how it went. We would break it down, hole by hole. But at the core of our rela-

A warrior with his tools of the trade ready for combat.

Dad watches anxiously as Tiger prepares to hit his first shot in his first golf tournament at Navy Golf Course in Cypress, California.

Under the watchful eye of his Dad, Tiger works on his golf swing.

tionship was the promise that whatever happened, Mom and I loved him for the person he was, not the golfer he was trying to be. I would take him to the first tee and say, "Son, I want you to know I love you no matter how you do. Enjoy yourself."

He had no fear of making a mistake. After hitting a terrific

Practice, practice, practice, as Tiger works on his game in the family garage.

drive, I would ask Tiger afterwards what he was concentrating on.

Tiger would answer: "Where I wanted my ball to go, Daddy."

That's when I knew how good he was going to be.

By second grade Tiger already had played in, and won, his first international tournament, against youngsters from all over the world. When he was 13, Tiger went undefeated in southern

California junior golf events—30 tournaments in all, most with fields of more than 100 players.

When he was 11 years and 11 months old, he finally beat me at a round of golf.

It was on November 28, 1987, to be precise. Tiger shot a 71 and I shot a 72 at the Long Beach Navy Golf Course. Our group that afternoon included Clark Canfield, Rick Bird and Bill Thompson. Tiger shot a 39 on the front nine and a 32 on the back nine. His round included four birdies.

I had two reactions. First, I was mad. I had just been beaten by an 11-year-old. I had never really focused on competing against Tiger, because I always wanted him to succeed. But now he was spending every waking hour competing against me. Every round we played, he always knew exactly how many strokes he was behind. I never paid attention . . . until that fateful day as we approached the 15th hole and he said, "Daddy," and these words still ring in my ears today: "I am ahead of you."

I said, "What?" It wasn't possible . . . was it? I wasn't keeping close track of the scores, although I knew that I was shooting well, on an even par pace. But sure enough, he was ahead of me. I freely admit I tried like heck to beat Tiger on those last three holes, but I couldn't catch him. He beat me that day, and I have never beat him again. Never. And don't laugh, you could be next!

My second reaction that afternoon literally changed my own outlook on golf. Now my score no longer seemed important. The only important factor was what Tiger shot. As a result, I lost my own competitive instincts and urges to win. Now I was perfectly content just to be on a golf course, to play just for fun, to watch my son master his own game.

Contrary to what you might hear, golf was never forced on Tiger. He was a typical teenager, and we encouraged him to get involved in other sports and activities, to develop his friendships instead of golfing all the time. He was always so tense

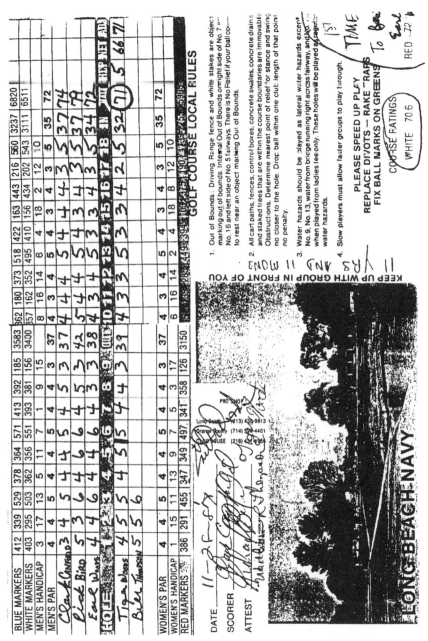

Tiger's winning scorecard from November 11, 1987—the first time he beat me at a round of golf. It was around this time that he started calling me "Pop," and the nickname has stuck ever since.

and competitive on the golf course. I once asked him, "Why don't you just relax out here and enjoy the birds and the flowers and the sunshine and the clouds?"

He looked at me strangely and said, "That's how I enjoy myself, by shooting low scores."

I said, "OK, I will never mention that again." And I never have.

There were days when he would get frustrated, like any golfer, and he would say, "I don't feel like playing."

I would tell him: "Well, quit. Jump on your bike and go over and see your friend Michael." So he would go over to Michael's house and play Nintendo or Ping-Pong. That would last for about two days. By the third day he would be back around the house hitting golf shots all over the place. By the fourth day he was back on the golf course.

I always taught him to listen to his body. It is okay to put the clubs away. "Nobody is forcing you to play this game," I told him. But the fact remained that he simply loved to play.

Most people do not realize what a tremendous athlete Tiger could have been in other sports if he had pursued them as vigorously as he did the game of golf. He was a prolific soccer player. He was a natural switch-hitter in baseball; when Tiger was two years old, I was pitching the ball in the air to him, and he was hitting it over the fence. He was a gifted runner. And he could kick a football even when he was little. But he never took up these sports: "They interfere with my golf," he said.

When Tiger was a little kid, he was playing in a pickup football game down at the park, right down the street from our house. A couple of hours later, his friends came carrying Tiger down the street toward home. He had been knocked out. The other kids told us Tiger had gone to field a punt and ran smack-dab into a tree, knocking himself out cold. So the kids came dragging him home. He loved playing contact sports, and he would come home with his knees and elbows skinned up playing tackle football in a parking lot. He thought nothing of it. He enjoyed it.

When he was in his first year of junior high school, I encouraged him to go out for track. He went out for the cross-country team, and within three weeks he was the No. 2 runner on the squad. But he only ran for one season before quitting. He said it interfered with his golf.

Tiger is a beautiful runner. If you think he has a beautiful golf swing, you should see him run. It is the essence of fluidity. He has a long stride, and he has exceptional speed. His head never moves a fraction of an inch, no matter how fast he is running. He is just so graceful, reminiscent of the way Jesse Owens ran, although Jesse Owens was shorter and more muscular and wasn't as aesthetically pretty to watch. He was muscular and dynamic, like a quarter horse. Tiger is like a thoroughbred, with his long legs. He would have been a natural 400-meter guy. Poetry in motion.

As a golfer, Tiger has a competitive drive that you find in very few athletes in any sport. He is not in awe of anyone. It took an experience early in his life to begin establishing that toughness.

It occurred when Tiger was 11 years old, at the Junior World Championships in San Diego. He had just jumped up from the 10-and-under category to the 11- and 12-year-old category. In the first round of the first day, Tiger was paired with a 12-year-old kid who was about six feet tall, 195 pounds. Tiger was still a little bitty shrimp. The other kid proceeded to drive the green on the first hole. Tiger went into a funk, and never came out, even though he beat the guy. I just couldn't reach him. No matter how I tried to communicate with him throughout the entire tournament, he remained distant, preoccupied. He was someplace else.

It wasn't until we got home that he finally opened up. "Dad, I was scared," he belatedly admitted.

I asked, "What were you scared about?"

"Did you see that guy on the first hole drive the green? He was so big!" said Tiger.

I realized then that we were facing a moment that could have great significance in his life. So I said, "What about that guy?"

"He was so huge and strong. He drove the green," Tiger answered.

"Okay. Did he par the hole?" I asked.

"Yes," Tiger said.

"Did you par the hole?"

"Yes," said Tiger.

"Did you beat him?"

"Yes," Tiger responded, finally realizing the point. Tiger learned that day that golf is not a game that rewards size and strength.

Then he said: "Dad, I promise you no one will ever intimidate me again in my life."

Now Tiger is not intimidated by any golfer. He has never forgotten that lesson—and he never will.

If there was any secret to Tiger's early success, it was his incredible ability to respond to pressure: He never felt any. He just handled it.

By his teens, Tiger had played with Sam Snead and was presented a tournament trophy by Lee Trevino. He had played with Greg Norman, Jack Nicklaus and John Daly. Tiger is the youngest person ever to have played in a PGA Tour event (at 16 years and two months, in the 1992 Los Angeles Open); the youngest ever and the first black to win the U.S. Amateur (when he was 18, four years younger than Bobby Jones when he won his first Amateur, a year younger than Nicklaus when he won his); the first male ever to win three U.S. Juniors; the first male to win the Junior and the Amateur. And the list goes on and on.

Tiger was the first young man to win three USGA Juniors, all in dramatic fashion. He won in Orlando, on the 19th hole; in

Milton, Massachusetts, on the 18th; in Portland, on the 19th, after being two down with two to play and making two birdies—one on a remarkable fairway bunker shot.

Before he captured the U.S. Amateur on the Stadium course of the TPC at Sawgrass, I whispered into Tiger's ear, "Let the legend grow." Down six holes in the final match, Tiger roared back, making two birdies in the last three holes—including a 139-yard wedge to the island-green 17th that stayed out of the water by three feet. He won 2 up. It is considered the greatest comeback in the tournament's 100-year history.

You have to be tough to win consistently, and there is no quit in Tiger. Part of that is inborn, I'm sure, and part of it is due to certain examples of toughness he has seen in me.

One day, Tiger and I were going to be partners in a golf tournament. The morning of the tournament, I was feeding his German shepherd and reached out to the dog with some food in my hand. That dog bit me so hard its fang tooth went right through my middle finger. I have the scar to this day. The puncture wound went all the way through to the nail on the other side.

I was screaming, blood was all over the place, and the dog was acting all apologetic for taking a chunk out of my hand. I finally put some peroxide and ice on it with a bandage around it to stop the bleeding.

Tiger was clearly worried . . . about making our tee-time: "Pop, we've got a tee-time in 45 minutes."

I said, "OK, let's go."

"How are you going to play?" Tiger asked in amazement.

"When the going gets tough, the tough get going," I said, biting my lip.

To swing the club, I had to keep the middle finger of my right hand off the shaft. Not an easy trick, believe me. Yet I made that adjustment all day. Whenever my hand would start bleeding a little, I would take out some bandages and Tiger would re-dress it. It did indeed look ugly. This is the toughness that Tiger saw in me. He knows that when I talk about tough-ness it's from my own experience, and not just lip service I have given him over the years.

Mark my word. I see the day that Tiger could be winning golf tournaments by 10 strokes. He always wants to dominate, and that goes back to my father's philosophy, which I taught to Tiger: "When you've got the sonofabitch down, stomp on him."

Those were his exact words. I taught Tiger to show no mercy. And that is the way he approaches it. That way, he has no comfort zone. And that is also why he is so tough in match-play golf.

I didn't have to pass on to him the love of winning, because that was always there. He always wanted to win. But I did pass on to him the meaning of sportsmanship, being able to lose gracefully. I reinforced in him that as long as you did the best you could, you could be confident that you didn't lose, but someone else won. And that it was okay for someone else to win, as long as you gave your best. Many times I have told him: "You are not perfect, neither am I. That's why I make mistakes when I hit the ball. You are entitled to make mistakes, as well."

But Tiger remains a perfectionist. His degree of tolerance is considerably less than mine. It always has been that way. He just cannot seem to accept mediocrity.

What made Tiger such an outstanding golfer at such a young age? First of all, Tiger's swing is natural. It is not a learned behavior. It is a natural function. So he is always free to swing. Then he was blessed with the flexibility of his back. And you combine those two with his natural athletic talents and his eye-hand coordination, and it makes for a dynamite combination.

Tiger learned through trial and error, and he intuitively did the right things. This was substantiated by competent instruction, by his professionals and myself. We would coordi-nate what we were teaching Tiger, so we would all be on the same page. We didn't want him to receive conflicting information. His first golf teacher, Rudy Duran, and I were very careful about that. And as Tiger developed, the coordination with Rudy continued, and Tiger flourished. Now, of course, Butch Harmon works with Tiger. Butch was critical to our plan to take Tiger's natural talent and enhance it so that he could excel at the professional level. And it has worked.

But through all the teaching, training and coaching, my operative theme for teaching Tiger the game of golf was fun. We would compete, and we would work hard, but we always had fun. Without that, we would not have the relationship we have today, the respect and trust. I earned that from him. There is a bond and a private space between us that we can open up and say whatever we want to say. Tiger is never afraid to confide in me about his fears or concerns. That is because the truth comes easily for us. Tiger knows I never judge him and I will always listen. I never tell him to do something; I will give him information

Four-year-old Tiger takes a break from practice with his first pro teacher Rudy Duran at Heartwell Golf Club in Long Beach, California.

Tiger, I told you your clubs are just too short to fit on a golf cart.

and let him make a choice. He has done that very well.

Somewhere along the line, you do things for your child that are so good, so right, and you can only hope that your son or daughter understands what you've done for him or her. I am so blessed that Tiger is mature enough to acknowledge to me his appreciation for our beautiful relationship. A parent can't ask for anything more. Those are defining moments in a relationship. Those are the moments when you look at your child and know you have raised a good, good person. After all, that is what this whole exercise is about—raising a good person. Please, please never forget that!

● ●

Chapter Five

THE BIG PICTURE

DAD, CAN WE TALK?"

That's how the dialogue would start, my cue that Tiger needed to have a private and personal chat session with me when he was younger.

The marvelous line of communication we had established early on always seemed to put Tiger at ease when he came to me to talk about any of a variety of topics. Nothing was off limits. He trusted me implicitly with his feelings, his insecurities, his dreams. That was the derivative of a unique bond we had forged over time, a direct reflection of our high level of mutual trust and respect.

Tiger would come to my bedroom and ask if we could talk, and I would say, "Sure." At which point I would set the newspaper down, turn the television off, or the radio. Whatever I was reading or working on stopped. Total attention was focused on him. From the outset, I established a policy that whenever Tiger wanted to talk to me, everything else came to a halt.

Sometimes Tiger would close the door, sometimes he would not. Then Tiger would lie on the floor and get comfortable. I would stretch out on the bed and say, "Okay, what's on your mind? What's going on in your life?"

We couldn't even see each other, but we could feel each other's presence, hear each other's voices rising out of nowhere. Perhaps that is why it worked so well.

Initially, our talks usually began with a serious tone. Sometimes Tiger would present a hypothetical circumstance, and I knew darn well he was talking about a situation involving himself. Frequently, we would share a nervous laugh. There would be times when his voice would crack, and although I could not see his face, I knew he must be on the verge of crying. On other occasions he would collapse into the silliness of a little kid. I know there were times that I cried—both tears of joy and pain. Expressions of honest emotions were never forbidden between us. Those were cherished moments a parent can never forget. And these sessions continued when we were on the road at tournaments.

Often I would act as his counselor or adviser regarding problems or decisions he was mulling over. Other times I simply would act as a sounding board for observations Tiger had made. Never was I judgmental in my responses. That was crucial. I tried to be a good listener and provide information that Tiger could use to make the best choices available. In a sense, I suppose I was a part of his conscience.

Tiger wasn't the only one who benefited from our talks. They also helped me understand the inquisitive mind of a child, while reminding me of my own priorities, giving me perspective on what was most important in my life. Too often adults get caught up in the hectic day-to-day routine without ever focusing on the bigger, more important long-range picture. Tiger has always had a knack for looking at life with a wide-angle lens. That is a quality that I pray he always will retain.

To our family, the big picture became Tiger's extraordinary ability, and how to nurture it. The reality was that Tiger's early golf career was going to be costly, and on our relatively modest income, it was going to take some sacrifices and creative financing so that he could continue to compete, learn and grow. Of course, we were more than willing to sacrifice our personal and economic situations so that Tiger could do what he needed to do. We weren't necessarily sacrificing so that he could become a professional golfer; we just wanted to be there for our son and to facilitate his happiness. And golf was most certainly making him happy.

Tida and I never discussed the money we spent on Tiger's golf trips or other related expenses, which were considerable. Not once did we quarrel. Tida and I had an agreement when Tiger was born that she would stay home and take care of Tiger during the day, and I would go out and earn the living. We agreed that Tiger was the top priority. Everything was geared toward his development.

For most families, summers and holidays meant vacations,

Daredevil Tiger works out at Sea World in San Diego, California.

togetherness. To us, summers and holidays were filled with tournaments. At Christmastime, I would travel with Tiger to Miami for the Junior Invitational Golf Tournament. On Thanksgiving Day, we would go to Tucson, Arizona, for their major event. We spent Easters at the Woodlands Tournament in Texas. The hardest part was that Tida couldn't even go with us; we couldn't afford the traveling expense of two parents. So those trips were never considered family vacations; we were there to win a tournament. There was no sightseeing or taking it easy. There was work to be done.

The financial sacrifices we had to make as a family to keep Tiger participating in national golf tournaments were substantial, but I wanted to make sure Tiger had every possible opportunity to succeed as much as the kids from wealthier families who supported their youngsters. So I took out a revolving home equity loan on our home, which was used each summer for expenses, then paid back during the winter. That meant we were broke in the winter. Looking back now, sometimes I wonder how we made it. Tida and I didn't take a vacation for over 20 years. But the experience just shows what you can accomplish through frugality and determination. I figure it cost me between $25,000 to $30,000 a year to enter Tiger into national tournaments, including the cost of my traveling with him everywhere. I'm sure there were other parents who were comfortable sending their kids without adult chaperones, but Tida and I were not among them. I did not want my child out there by himself on the road, unsupervised. I wanted to be there with him. And Tida insisted that I accompany him, as well. Boy, did she ever!

We made it through those tough financial times by being at the right place at the right time, saving money when we could, and anticipating costs. Also, the considerable help of others made it all possible for Tiger to continue his pursuit of excellence.

But the road to success has occasional potholes in it, and Tiger's path was no different. Tiger experienced many obsta-

Boogie board time! Let's hit the beach, Mom! Tida and Tiger head out for the Pacific Ocean to catch some waves.

Tiger learns to square dance in grade school in 1987.

cles—many of them racially motivated, both subtle and overt—
at an early age, beginning at our local military course in our
hometown of Cypress, California, where we moved after a year
in Los Alamitos.

Near where he grew up (and where I still live) in Cypress,
California, there is a military golf course where I played after
my retirement from the service. Now, picture this: The average
age of the members was about 63. If you trace back to their military duty, you will find that most of these guys were in the
military at a time when blacks were not even trusted with
weapons; blacks could be stewards and cooks, and that was
about it. That was their experiential background with blacks in
the military forces.

Then I showed up. They used to call me "Sgt. Brown": It
was inconceivable to them that a black guy could rise above the
rank of sergeant. And this "playful" routine went on for a long
time. Until one night at the bar, the bartender finally said,
"Hold it up, gentlemen. Just a moment. I want to introduce you
to Lt. Colonel Earl Woods. Ex-Green Beret, two-time veteran of
Vietnam!"

Dead silence. I outranked all of them. And to make things
worse (for them), I had athletic talent and a single-digit handicap of about one. I would win all the big first-place money in
the member-guest tournaments and in the member-member
tournaments. So, they changed the rules creating three competition brackets by handicap, effectively reducing the prize
money to be won to one-third.

But above all, I had the nerve to have this precocious kid.
They couldn't handle that, either. Tiger was so good, and so
cute. He was picture-perfect. The head PGA pro allowed him to
go out on the golf course at the age of three, because he was
that good.

Then the head pro started to get complaints that Navy regulations said that you had to be 10 years old to play a military

golf course. Are there really Navy regulations on how old someone has to be to play on the course? I have no idea, because they have never, ever shown them to me. In fact, when Tiger went to San Diego to play in the Junior World Tournament, we played at a Navy course where the age limit was eight years old. So it was not a regulation. It was an arbitrary number thrown in our face to keep Tiger off the course in Cypress, selectively enforced. The result: They pulled Tiger's playing privileges.

Then when Tiger was four, the club got a new pro. I asked him one day, "Do you think Tiger could play this golf course?"

He said, "I don't know. He's pretty young."

I said, "Let me ask you a question. If you played with him on a regular course and you gave him a stroke a hole, and Tiger hits from where you hit and he beats you . . . do you think he can play this course?"

The pro laughed and said, "Hell yes."

I said, "Let's make it honorable. I will bet you a dollar he beats you."

He said, "There is no way that a four-year-old kid is going to beat me at a stroke a hole."

So we played nine holes, and Tiger beat him by three strokes. And the pro had no choice but to let Tiger play the course. And he paid me the dollar.

Well, complaints came again, the complainers going over the pro's head. And when they pulled Tiger's playing privileges again and said he couldn't play there anymore, I said, "Tiger, we don't need this place," and he hasn't returned to this day.

That's when we left the Navy course and he began playing regularly at Heartwell Golf Park, a par 3 course in Long Beach. That became Tiger's home course. The head pro there was Rudy Duran, an ex-PGA Tour player. It was Tida who took Tiger to Long Beach and asked if her four-year-old son could play on their course. Rudy said, "Well, let's take him out to the driving range and see how he does."

The rest is history.

"Tiger was like a little shrunken-down pro," Rudy said. "Tiger can play here anytime he wants."

So Tiger grew up in their junior club. They had tournaments every Saturday afternoon not—at 4 o'clock or 5 o'clock in the afternoon, after most of the adults were finishing for the day, but at noon. This man really supported the junior program. He had 20 kids, of all ages up to 18, and he worked diligently with each one.

Tiger started working with Rudy at the age of four, and within four years, at age eight, he was club champion. And from that group of 20 kids came three U.S. Boys Junior champions, three U.S. Amateur men's national champions, and a women's U.S. Amateur champion, Amy Fruhwirth, who is now on the LPGA Tour. And there were a whole bunch of collegiate golfers and subsequent PGA club pros that came from that same group of 20 kids.

In an ironic way, Tiger's road to success began with the bigotry and closed-mindedness he encountered at the Navy golf course. And it culminated in total acceptance at the par 3 Heartwell Golf Park, where Tiger learned on a golf course that was his size. That is where Tiger learned to develop his short game: He couldn't reach the greens on those par 3s when he was three or four years old, so he developed his short game, chipping and putting. And he was never bored, because he had a system of always taking a tee shot and then an approach shot. It was all his size. And that's what is so beautiful about it. Strange how unwelcome, unforeseen circumstances can shape our lives.

Now, who was wise enough to know that Tiger should be there? It wasn't me. Why was he at Heartwell Golf Park, on a par 3 golf course? It wasn't my decision. I am very good, but I am not that good. Things have always happened for a reason in the lives of Tiger and me. It was just meant to be. We had to wade through the bigots to find the right place for us. We were playing through.

From that time on, things really started to happen, and Tiger moved beyond the stage of "cute little kid who can golf." Now he was being recognized by the serious golf community. Renowned golf pro Byron Nelson had watched Tiger's progression as a child, and said in 1997: "The first time I saw Tiger play, he was the best 15-year-old golfer I had ever seen. He was the best 16-year-old, 17-, 18-, 19-, 20- and now 21-year-old golfer. I've never seen anything like it."

That was high praise coming from a golfer of Nelson's esteem.

From the time he was five years old, Tiger was aware he was special; the media attention he received made it virtually impossible for him not to come to that early realization. Our neighbors knew about his talent by virtue of the newspaper articles about him, the television shows he appeared on, the tournaments he won. So it was not a secret by any stretch of the

Commander Jay Brunza, USN, congratulates 13-year-old Tiger for winning his third consecutive Junior World at San Diego, California. Now retired from service, Brunza has been Tiger's sports psychologist for many years.

Fifteen-year-old Tiger with his friend Mark O'Meara at Isle Wortk Country Club in Orlando, Florida, where Tiger would eventually make his home. Their friendship continues to this day.

imagination. But to us, and to our community, he was just a happy kid with a big heart. I'm not aware of any jealousy emanating from other families in the neighborhood, just pride. Tiger used to stand on our front lawn and hit lightweight plastic golf balls across the street onto my neighbor's lawn. He would pick out a bush and hit balls at the target over and over again. None of the neighbors ever complained. Perhaps it was because Tiger was so precise with his shots that he never broke anything. I can still see him standing in our backyard hitting balls over the roof of our house, into a tree well.

So you see, Tiger was already quite a celebrity by the time he reached Western High School in Anaheim, California, where he made the varsity golf team as a freshman and proceeded to thoroughly dominate the high school ranks under the tutelage of his coach, Don Crosby. But he was quiet and humble about his notoriety, which helped him blend in easily to the high school scene. His high school included a pretty good racial mixture of whites, blacks, Hispanics and Asians. There were a few gangs in his school, but they left Tiger alone out of respect for his athletic ability.

But despite his efforts to blend in, he still managed to snag the attention of a group that would spend several years making Tiger's life hell. I speak, of course, of the NCAA.

Much has been written about Tiger's monolithic battles with the NCAA, the almighty governing body that regulates what student athletes can and cannot do. Most young athletes aren't confronted by the NCAA until they're on their way to college, but Tiger was "lucky." His battle started even before Tiger was under their jurisdiction. It started when he was still in high school.

From the start, it seemed that Tiger's conflict with the NCAA was a battle of strong wills and arbitrary principles all the way. Two years before he would go to college, Big Canyon Country Club in California decided to extend to him an invitation to be an honorary member. Tiger graciously accepted that invitation. Actually, I accepted for him, and our family became members. As a matter of protocol, Tiger notified the United States Golf Association, just to make sure he wasn't in violation of anything under their domain that would prevent him from participating in any of their sanctioned events.

Well, all of a sudden, the USGA decided it had to contact the NCAA. I said, "Wow, wait a minute. Why is that? Tiger is not under their jurisdiction. They have no control over what he does right now."

I was stunned to think that an organization such as the NCAA, which has no jurisdiction over high school student-athletes, would have power over them before they even got to college. That is when I realized we were going to have a fight on our hands with the NCAA when it came to Tiger's high school activities. They ultimately ruled that if it was okay by his sanctioning organization (the USGA), it was acceptable to them. I could have told them that in the first place. What a blatant use of arbitrary power. They would later get their revenge while Tiger was attending Stanford. They couldn't stop his being a member of Big Canyon, because that was granted by the USGA prior to his attending college.

In the end, the USGA approved the membership in the Big Canyon Country Club based on the fact that Tiger had achieved a significant event by winning the U.S. Junior Amateur championship, and the club was justified in offering this to him. No problem. The California State High School Athletic Association was checked also, and they had no objection to the club's offer. We finally made it through the bureaucratic obstacle course. But the episode served to foreshadow our future encounters with the seemingly omnipotent NCAA. And there would be plenty.

Ho-hum, another Junior World title in 1991. At age 15, Tiger was the youngest ever to win the 15- to 18-year-old age bracket.

The first shot on the first tee at the Los Angeles Open in 1992.

Tiger was a very good student, always keeping up with his studies and making the honor roll in high school every year. Tida should receive great credit for assuring that Tiger stayed on target when it came to schoolwork. She had a very simple rule: "No schoolwork, no golf." And Tiger bought into this completely.

Her Asian cultural influence on Tiger's upbringing was critical in his quick maturation. Tida always preached humility, determination, respect, spirituality, honesty and diligence in

High school student Tiger Woods warms up on the driving range at the Rivera Country Club for the Los Angeles Open.

Tiger and I participate in our now-famous hug to celebrate winning a third straight U.S. Junior Amateur in August 1993 at Waverly Country Club in Portland, Oregon. Jay Brunza, left, and Tiger's opponent Ryan Armour observe.

The sign tells the final results in extra holes as Tiger is the winner of the U.S. Junior Amateur for the third straight time.

her daily interaction with Tiger. The devotion between Tiger and his mother underscores his insistence not to deny his racial heritage. To this day he wears a heavy golf chain with the replica of a gold Buddha around his neck, a symbol of the Buddhist religion he embraces. And you might say Tiger continues to wear his feelings about his mother on his sleeve.

For all of Tiger's wonderful characteristics, the one thing we were never able to change was his tendency to be a perfectionist. He demanded a lot of himself as a boy, and he still demands a lot today. When Tiger was a teenager, one of the things his sports psychologist had to work with him on was his intolerance for mistakes.

"Stop beating up on yourself on the golf course," he would tell Tiger.

Even today, when Tiger feels he's made an error, you can see him on television coming off a green in disgust. He will be flailing his arms, contorting his face, talking to himself. But this is his method; it seems to work for him. I could suggest to him:

"Let's drop that habit and change your ways." But I have to ask myself, Do you want him to be a carefree, mediocre robotic golfer, or do you want him to be an intense great golfer? It seems impossible to reach a compromise on those personality traits when it comes to Tiger's golf game; it is his disposition and his competitive edge that give him the ability to play better when he is angry. Not many people have that attribute, but he does. I have talked to Tiger about showing his emotions on the golf course, and I have virtually come around to endorsing his actions. Now I say: "Don't hold your emotions in, because they become ticking time bombs that eventually will explode. Let your emotions out. But don't allow your emotions to interfere with your next shot." Boy, did we work hard on this over the years.

I'm sure Tiger learned a lot about showing his emotions from watching and listening to me. Throughout his entire childhood, Tiger and I maintained a central line of communication, always based on openness, caring, and plenty of emotion. As he grew older and we were traveling together to amateur golf tournaments around the country, we had so many wonderful insightful conversations. We would stay in the same room, so we could talk one-on-one, with none of the interruptions that usually distract parents from focusing their full attention on their children. As he got older, the talks became more comprehensive and complicated. Such is life, I suppose. But we always had those talks, the exchange of ideas and feelings. Our sessions weren't necessarily related to problems he was having, or about golf. Tiger is just a very curious person, and I always have encouraged him to question things. I would tell him: "Don't accept every word that is written in the newspaper or spoken on the television. Find out for yourself whether the information is correct or applicable to you and your situation. Even question your teachers and instructors in school if you need to know something."

As he matured, Tiger began questioning me more, too, and

I encouraged that. I'm always willing to admit my mistakes, and I freely admitted them to my son when he called me on something he didn't understand. It humanized me in his eyes in a way that improved our relationship; he had the maturity to realize that I wasn't the holier-than-thou, know-it-all parent. I was a guy who knew a lot about a lot of things, but I was willing to admit when I didn't have all of the answers. I tried to set the example for Tiger by getting information I didn't have, by reading and investigating. Then I would get back to him with my findings. Tiger emulates that process of researching facts to this day.

As a parent, you hope you raise your child to be independent, to make good decisions, to determine what is best for himself. And so when Tiger came to the point in his life when he had to choose a college, I felt it was a decision he needed to explore for himself. Tida and I had spent 17 years providing the

Tiger and caddie Jay Brunza watch the opponent's ball in flight as Tiger defends his U.S. Amateur championship in Portland, Oregon.

Tiger takes off the blinders at his home in Cypress, California, and finds a surprise party celebrating his winning the 1994 U.S. Amateur Championship. Tida, who organized the event, shares in the moment.

environment for positive personal development, giving him the tools that he'd need to be a successful adult. Now it was his turn to show what he could do with them.

Tiger had been recruited by numerous colleges, all undoubtedly exhilarated by the thought of getting this phenomenal young golfer in their athletic programs. He was most heavily recruited by Stanford, Arizona State, Virginia, Arizona, and Nevada–Las Vegas, and after a lot of consideration, Tiger eliminated Virginia due to its East Coast location, and Arizona

A celebration cake for the 1994 U.S. Amateur champion Tiger Woods.

Tida, Tiger and I enjoy the moment as the city of Cypress, California, Tiger's hometown, honors his 1994 U.S. Amateur title.

The city of Cypress presents Tiger with its key.

State and Arizona, because he didn't want to go to school in the desert. That left UNLV, because he admired the coach, and Stanford.

I decided not to go on the recruiting trips with Tiger. I told him to gather enough information so that he could justify his decision based upon solid facts, rather than his emotions, because his mother and I had veto rights on his selection. We were the committee that had to approve his choice. So Tiger was very aware that he had to obtain enough information to convince us of his selection.

First he made his trip to UNLV, where he was very impressed with the golfing facility. Later, the athletic director told me that Tiger asked the most succinct and piercing questions of any athletic recruit he had ever talked to. I was proud of that, because I knew Tiger was doing his homework.

But as soon as Tiger visited Stanford, he said, "I knew I

Tiger and his dog Joey pose near the "wall of fame" at his home in Cypress, California.

was home." He had made his choice. And when he came back home and said he had selected Stanford, he began to tell us about all the important aspects of the school. He talked about the academics, which was just as important to me, if not more important, and I said, "OK, fine. Tell me more."

If it had simply been a matter of choosing the school with the best golfing facility, it would have been UNLV. That would have been the best place for him to cultivate his game. But his

Tiger celebrates for the last time before sending the U.S. Junior Amateur trophy back to the USGA. After winning it three times, it was like giving up an old friend.

game did not need a great deal of cultivating, and Stanford provided the best combination of an unrivaled academic environment and competitive golf program.

When it was time for Tiger to go to college, I asked him, "Do you want me to come?"

He answered, "No, Pop, that's OK. I can handle it."

I said, "OK, fine. You know that anytime you want me to be there with you, I will."

My favorite trophy, the Haverman, awarded to the U.S. Amateur champion. We kept it for three straight years.

And that was it. It was time for me to pull back, and I did just that. I gave him complete space to learn and grow on his own. In spirit, he knew I was there. It was time for Tiger to learn from his own experiences; he had learned as much as he could from mine.

• •

Chapter Six

PAR FOR THE COURSE

WHEN TIGER WENT off to college, I told Tida, "You know, he's gone. He will never be a resident of this house again in his entire life."

She said, "What do you mean?"

"Well, he'll only be a visitor from now on," I said. And that is exactly what happened: He went straight from collegian to international superstar. And he never came home for his stuff. He left his computer, he left his TV, he left his Nintendo, he left all of his clothes. He left money. When he turned professional, his new sponsors provided him with most of what he needed, and whatever they didn't provide, he had plenty of money to buy. So he left everything right where it was and never came back for it.

I knew from the day he left for Stanford that he was traveling a road that would not lead him back to Cypress, California. But that road was going to take him places no one had ever been, so I wasn't necessarily sorrowful when he left. I do admit to feeling a bit melancholy and nostalgic. I will confess to that much. I tried to be positive about it, though, and when he departed that fall and I turned him over to the Stanford golf coach, Wally Goodwin, I said, "Free at last!" And everybody laughed. It took some of the sting out of the moment.

Tida viewed the departure of her only child to Stanford as a less symbolic and more emotional event than I did, although the school was situated only about a one-hour flight up the California coast from our home.

Tiger's departure was a milestone for which I had been preparing him for many years. It was a rite of passage, a transitional moment. I had no doubt he was suited to make the move. When your son is able to shoot a 48 for nine holes at the age of three, you begin to believe he is capable of accomplishing practically anything by the time he is 18.

My mother would have been so proud to see her beaming, wide-eyed grandson step onto that charming, picturesque college campus, with a world of opportunities before him. Tiger loved Stanford as an academic institution, as well as for what it represented. He would say, "Pop, I am at home. Everybody is special at Stanford.

"There's a guy in my dorm who already has taken every mathematics course that Stanford offers, and he is a freshman studying the theoretical level of math! And we have another student here who put together a computer out of parts. And it worked. Everybody is smart here, Pop, and everybody is special," Tiger said. "I don't feel like I am out in left field. I feel very comfortable."

So comfortable, in fact, that I didn't even go to visit Tiger at Stanford until the spring of his freshman year, when I went to watch him in a golf tournament. I wanted him to be totally free, and he appreciated that opportunity to grow, and took advantage of it. He was in a wonderful academic environment, and his mind was totally exposed to so many new ideas and concepts.

I already thought Tiger was pretty great before he went off to school, but when he returned home for Christmas during his freshman year, I was just amazed. Like many young kids, Tiger had been hooked on television; I was always trying to get him to read more when he was in high school. Stanford broke him of his TV habit within a month. Now he was bringing home books that he had been reading just for his sheer enjoyment, in addition to the books he had been assigned to read by professors. I do have to give Tiger some credit for his new attitude: When he went away to college he was wise enough to leave his television set and computer at home. He realized he was going to Stanford to learn and broaden his academic horizons, not lay around watching TV or playing computer games.

For the most part, Tiger enjoyed the collegiate experience, and he cultivated some wonderful friendships. In many ways, he acted like a typical freshman, and for a parent, that was joyous and wonderful to see. Of course, I missed seeing Tiger around the house and accompanying him on the road to golf tournaments. It was a real transition for me, and like many parents who watch their child leave the nest, I felt a void in my day-to-day life. Yet Tiger and I knew that we knew we were there for each other in spirit. And in the end, that is what mattered most.

However, living away from home for the first time was not without its occasional tense moments for Tiger. During his freshman year, for instance, Tiger was mugged at knifepoint behind his school dormitory; he was confronted by a man with a knife when he returned from an on-campus party. The assailant took Tiger's watch and gold chain and hit him in the jaw with the knife handle, knocking him to the ground. Fortunately, Tiger escaped serious injury, but it was pretty frightening.

But the positive experiences far exceeded the negative ones for Tiger during his two-year college career. Not only was his golf game thriving, but he was doing well academically, too. And, most important, he was learning lessons about the world and his place in it, lessons that would prepare him for the incredible life he was about to lead.

Remember Shoal Creek? The private, all-white club in Birmingham, Alabama, made national headlines and caused tremendous debate during the days leading up to the 1990 PGA Championship being played there, when its founder said the club wouldn't be pressured into accepting blacks. The ensuing uproar caused the PGA and the USGA to establish a standard set of guidelines on membership policies for all courses involved with professional tournaments, and even Shoal Creek changed its policy. And in 1994, Stanford freshman Tiger Woods walked off that final green at Shoal Creek, a winner on the course that forever will be linked with golf's civil-rights awakening.

"I just went out and wanted to play well," Tiger said after his two-shot victory in the Jerry Pate National Intercollegiate tournament. In winning this tournament, he became the first golfer of color to do so.

Tiger would continue breaking down social barriers in the spring of his freshman year when he made his first trip as the U.S. Amateur champion to the exalted greens at Augusta, where he made the cut at the Masters. He finished way back in

Joey, Penny and Dad enjoy a leisurely moment in Tiger's room while he was away at Stanford.

the pack for him, when the final scores were tallied, but he impressed a lot of people with his driving. He averaged 311 yards on selected holes, ahead of pros Davis Love III and John Daly who averaged 306 and 297, respectively.

It was a tremendous thrill to be at the Masters, but Tiger was also learning quickly that the life of a high-profile athlete is not as easy as it might seem.

"It's not the glamorous life that you see on TV, the guys leading the tournament and winning all the time," Tiger told the media during the summer of his freshman year, at the Western Open at Cog Hill in Chicago; it was his first tournament since withdrawing from the U.S. Open two-and-a-half weeks earlier with a wrist injury.

"They don't see what happens the rest of the time when they're struggling or they're not playing or handling some little endorsement commitments that they have to do."

He had battled a variety of injuries, including surgery to remove benign tumors from his left knee, and a sprained ligament in his wrist, injured while he was swinging through the thick grass at the U.S. Open at Shinnecock Hills, forcing him to withdraw in the second round.

Tiger also was learning to handle increased media attention, and the press' preoccupation with his ethnic heritage. Tiger was widely referred to as "the first black golfer" to win the U.S. Amateur, and one of the very few African-Americans to play at Augusta National, site of the Masters. Tired of the racial labeling, Tiger issued a statement at the U.S. Open, saying: "The various media have portrayed me as African-American, sometimes Asian. In fact, I am both. The critical and fundamental point is that ethnic background . . . should not make a difference. Now with your cooperation I hope I can just be a golfer and a human being."

By the end of his freshman year, he was a veteran at handling the media crush and the pressures of college life. Unfortunately, Stanford and Tiger came up short in a bid for another NCAA title. Tiger missed a putt in a team playoff as Oklahoma State took the national championship from Stanford. It was a heartbreaking loss. Stanford would fall short again during his sophomore year. But Tiger did win the individual national collegiate title.

But of all the obstacles he encountered during his two year college career, none rocked him as hard and profoundly as those thrown in his face by the almighty NCAA.

I know there are those who think that Tiger turned professional after his sophomore year because he saw huge financial opportunities. Let me assure you, it was never our intention to do what so many young athletes are doing today, giving up their eligibility for huge professional contracts. My first priority for Tiger was, and has always been, his well-being and his growth as a person. But the astounding restraints placed on us by the NCAA forced me to reassess something I had believed throughout my entire life: that education came above every-

The 1994–95 Stanford golf team receives the first-place trophy at the Thousand Oaks Collegiate Invitational. L-R: Casey Martin, Steve Burdick, Will Yamagisawa, Tiger and Notah Begay. Coach Wally Goodwin directs the action.

thing. Somehow, the NCAA had forced us right out the door.

Soon after enrolling at Stanford, Tiger was offered privileges at the Olympic Golf Club in nearby San Francisco. It was the same home-away-from-home deal that the Big Canyon Club provided Tiger a couple years earlier while he was still in high school. Tiger would have somewhere to go and relax and play while he was at Stanford in Palo Alto, reasoned the club officials. They also wanted to make him an honorary member, just as Big Canyon had done while he was in high school.

By this point, as a college student, Tiger was under the jurisdiction of the National Collegiate Athletic Association, the governing body of several hundred college athletic programs throughout America, and we needed NCAA approval before we could accept the gracious offer. But there are procedures for these things. You don't contact the NCAA directly; you have to go through a compliance officer at Stanford. The compliance officer contacts the NCAA on your behalf. So we tendered a formal request for Tiger to be allowed to become an honorary member of Olympic Golf Club. The bid was denied. Big surprise.

We went back to the compliance officer and said, "Well, the same arrangement with Big Canyon was approved once before."

But the NCAA, again through the Stanford compliance officer, stated, "We didn't approve that arrangement, either."

The rules state in essence that no student athlete can receive any benefit that isn't available to the entire team. In other words, in order for us to accept the offer from the Olympic Golf Club, the invitation would have to be extended to the entire Stanford team. To be sure, that was not going to happen.

Now, we weren't talking about a free Porsche or wads of cash. We were talking about the use of a golf course, and the right to practice his sport freely. I felt that such a reaction by the NCAA to our request was a capricious, arbitrary use of power, and I didn't appreciate it.

The NCAA and its overzealous watchdogs would butt in selectively, in my opinion, to search for any violation in Tiger's actions. They hassled him when he changed his brands of golf balls and clubs. They questioned the publication of his Masters diaries in two golf publications, and suspended him for one day.

But none of this compared to the uproar over Tiger's now-famous dinner with golf great Arnold Palmer.

Tiger had the thrill of meeting Arnold when Tiger won his first U.S. Junior title at Bay Hill Country Club, and since then, Arnold had communicated off and on with him. Now, Tiger was an 18-year-old college freshman, and Arnold was going to play a Senior PGA event in Napa Valley, near Stanford. Tiger saw an opportunity to talk with him in person, get some personal advice from someone he deeply admired. People were beginning to tell Tiger that he was going to be a great ambassador for the game of golf, and he wanted to talk with Arnold about what that really meant, what responsibilities lay ahead for him. It was nothing more than a young college student seeking career advice from someone who had been at the very top, something any collegian must be entitled to do. Tiger didn't want anything material from Arnold. He just wanted to talk, to discuss what life was like for him when he was a young superstar on the PGA Tour.

So Arnold's secretary set up their meeting, and Tiger drove from San Francisco to Napa Valley. They met in the lobby of Arnold's hotel, where the restaurant had arranged for Tiger and Arnold to dine at a rather secluded corner table so that no one would disturb them. They had a very quiet dinner and a most productive, inspiring talk, about how Tiger could best become a responsible emissary of the game of golf, what the role would entail and what it means to be the top golfer in the world. Arnold was very supportive, very insightful.

Well, the check came and Arnold said, "I'll pay for it." Tiger then offered to give him a $25 check for his portion of the bill, but Arnold insisted, "No, no, I'll pay for it." And they went their separate ways.

So you can imagine Tiger's shock when someone showed him a newspaper headline breaking the story about his innocent dinner with Arnold. He was in Chicago playing in a tournament and doing a clinic for inner-city kids, arranged by Stanford, when his coach Wally Goodwin heard about this alleged NCAA violation. Upon returning to Stanford, Goodwin confronted Tiger.

"Tiger, did you have dinner with Arnold Palmer, and did you pay for your own bill?" he asked.

Tiger said, "No, Arnold paid the bill."

Tiger's coach immediately decided to suspend him, saying that Stanford would have to notify the NCAA of this. And that was that. His coach never bothered to ask any other pertinent questions, such as "Did you know Arnold before?" or "Was he a personal friend?" which are the extenuating circumstances that placed their meeting within the framework of the rules.

Tiger was scheduled to leave the next day for the All-America Tournament in El Paso, Texas, and the Stanford staff told him to go down there and that they would let him know the NCAA's decision. So Tiger went to Texas alone, with no one else from his school, not knowing whether he was going to play or not, believing he was suspended by the NCAA. And he waited, and waited.

Now, Tida became extremely agitated about the whole abomination. But once again, we are not allowed to talk directly to the NCAA. All we could do was attempt to talk to the compliance officer at Stanford. But to make matters more complicated, she had no obligation to speak to us, since we were merely the parents of a scholarship athlete. I had tried to establish a pleasant relationship with her earlier in the year so that I could maintain some dialogue with her throughout Tiger's stay at the university. We had developed a good rapport, but it wasn't the best of situations for either of us.

In the meantime, Tida had called several people in the media and told them about this apparent injustice directed at Tiger. Don't ever get Tida started by messing with her kid. The national press initiated some inquiries, and the issue snowballed into front page sports news. Finally, the NCAA, in its infinite wisdom, relented under all this scrutiny and announced: "We won't suspend him."

Now, Tiger was still down in Texas, where no one had taken a moment to tell him anything. Finally, some reporters got in touch with Stanford officials and asked, "Well, has Tiger been notified yet that he hasn't been suspended?"

"No," they replied.

So instead of being happy that he wasn't suspended, he was devastated to realize that he was the last to know his own fate. But true to form, he showed his mental toughness. He won the damn tournament.

The embarrassing incident left an indelible impression on Tiger, and I am sure that the ordeal was the catalyst that soured him on collegiate golf. It is all traceable to the NCAA, with a big assist from Stanford. He never again felt the same way about the Stanford golf program. In my mind, there seems to be a sort of paranoid fear of the NCAA by many schools around the country, and I suppose it's with good reason—the NCAA can shut you down with the wave of its rule book.

After the incident, Tida and I flew up to Stanford for a meeting with the athletic director (AD) and the coach to discuss the unfortunate misunderstanding. I told them: "You guys are scared to death of the NCAA. Why don't you stop having an organization run you, when it is supposed to be there to serve you? You should be in charge of it. It doesn't make any sense."

To his credit, the AD agreed. He said, "Well, I have friends in the NCAA. Do you want me to go back there when I visit them and talk to them about Tiger's incident?"

I said, "Yeah, go ahead. Suit yourself." I never got a formal or informal report on the results of his visit.

Tiger unleashes another long drive at Olympic Golf Club in San Francisco, California, as he competes as a Stanford sophomore in 1995.

Tiger gets assistance from Stanford teammate Notah Begay as he checks in for the 1995 Masters.

The 1995–96 Stanford golf team reflect on their 4th place finish at the NCAA tournament held at the Honors course in Tennessee.

Tiger calls it a night after attending the 1995 Sullivan Awards hosted by the U.S. Amateur Athletic Union held in Indianapolis, Indiana.

I think so many of the rulings and actions by the NCAA are unjust, arbitrary, a wavering abuse of power. They have the capability of ruining the lives of unprotected kids, along with the dreams of many parents who don't understand the reality of big-time collegiate sports. Some of the rules are so archaic, so complex, that they seem to have been designed merely to confuse.

For instance, years ago when Tiger was a junior amateur golfer still in high school, he and I started giving back to the game of golf by putting on clinics for inner-city kids all over the United States when we traveled to tournaments—New York, Chicago, Portland, Seattle, Dallas—and we weren't getting paid a dime for any of it. It was our attempt to give back to the community, by helping others. But when Tiger came under the jurisdiction of the NCAA, I had to refuse every one of those clinics. I would make a request to the compliance officer, who routed those requests to the NCAA. Invariably, every request came back disapproved. I was appalled—these were charitable clinics benefiting no one but the children in inner cities.

I finally asked what the regulations were, and the Stanford compliance officer sent me a copy of the guidelines.

The guidelines read that an NCAA scholarship athlete could not be involved in a clinic farther than 30 miles from his university or his domicile. Well, back in the days of the horse and buggy, 30 miles from a domicile referred to the distance a horse could travel in one day. That's how outdated those rules and regulations are.

Meanwhile, the regulations also stated that it was completely acceptable for the conference that Tiger played in to put on clinics, anywhere, anytime. And Stanford, in fact, used Tiger in their own golf clinics, such as the one in Chicago during the school year. Yet Tiger's own father couldn't conduct a nonprofit clinic even during the summer months.

I responded to the compliance officer: "In the summer months Tiger is not under the jurisdiction of the NCAA."

But the NCAA answered back: "Oh, yes he is. Once under the jurisdiction, always under the jurisdiction until he graduates or until he ceases his competitive athletic eligibility."

Until death do us part.

During the writing of my first book, *Training a Tiger*, while

Tiger was still under the jurisdiction of the NCAA and the USGA, I wrote to both organizations and asked what Tiger was permitted to do in support of my book. Could he be on the cover? Could he write the foreword? Could he pose for instructional pictures? Could he assist in the promotion? The USGA came back and said he could not be on the cover. He could write the foreword. He could pose for instructional pictures. But he could not promote the book. According to both the USGA and the NCAA regulations, his amateur status precluded Tiger from participating in these types of promotional ventures.

But the NCAA, through the Stanford compliance officer, responded with a very sarcastic reply, which I think is symptomatic and illustrative of their general attitude: They told me to take copious notes. In other words: We don't even have to dignify your request with a reply. We contain the power. We are not going to tell you what he can and cannot do. We own your kid. We can't tell you what to do, but we own your kid. And we can get at you through your kid.

I never did get a straight answer, other than a blanket "no way." That's what they were telling me. And there is no second court. There is no review. They knew they couldn't deny me the opportunity to make a living, but they could deny my son the right to participate with me, because he was their prisoner. The message was delivered loud and clear. And of course, there was nobody in that NCAA body that I could talk to directly. As a parent, I wasn't even permitted to call the organization.

The NCAA seemed determined to scrutinize Tiger because he was in the public limelight. Tiger wasn't trying to get away with anything. He was trying to do the best he could to comply with their confusing regulations. But he got nothing but grief at every turn. He was under constant surveillance, and, boy, did that ever taint his otherwise glorious collegiate experience. It drove Tiger right out of college.

Tiger had finally come to the realization that he needed to

change something. Now he was thinking: "You know, I am not going anywhere with these people while I'm in the college ranks. The NCAA is picking on me. They are watching me. They are looking for something wrong. And it is inevitable that one of these times they are going to get something on me they can embellish to bring me down. They will find something, and if they don't, they will probably invent it. Because who would know the difference?" And he finally said to himself: "I don't have to put up with this." Sound familiar? The Navy Golf Club, age four, all over again.

It took a lot more than megabuck sponsors such as Nike or Titleist to "show Tiger the money" before he decided to leave Stanford to turn pro. It took the abuse of his trust, which was unforgivable. You see, trust is a key characteristic in Tiger's makeup. And when it was broken at the collegiate level, he was devastated. They had tried to break his spirit. Tiger cannot live a lie, and he knew the whole system was a lie. He didn't want any part of it. He bailed.

The presidents of these universities have to reign, instead of the tail wagging the dog. I always have said that power corrupts. I don't care how well-intentioned you are when you start out . . . power corrupts.

And the schools lament that so many athletes are leaving college early. Well, *wake up*—the system is driving them out of college. These kids can't wait to get away from the NCAA.

It is an injustice that parents and their children who are student-athletes have to withstand a system like this to get an education and compete athletically. This should be a joyful time for them. But instead it amounts to servitude and jail. And what is the recourse? The recourse is to get up and say, "I am tired of it, I am fed up." And then what? They become totally embittered with the collegiate experience. The few athletes who can turn professional are the lucky ones. The unlucky ones are those who are stuck and can't get out. They have to put up with this out-of-control system. They are the silent majority forced to sit there and get ripped on every single day, with no recourse. These kids are indentured servants, trapped by the system. They see their universities making millions of dollars on their athletic talent, yet they don't have the money to make a phone call or do their laundry, nor do they have the right to go out and earn the money. I saw that potential financial trap coming, so I made sure Tiger had money in his bank account every month so that he could survive. I did not want my child to be subjected to that indignity.

We're a team. I support him and he knows I support him. He needs that support. But like any father of a 20-year-old, I had initial trepidations about seeing Tiger vault into the real world of professional athletics. Tiger, too, expressed concern about turning pro. After all, his record in the 17 professional events he had played in as an amateur was not spectacular. He had made the cut just seven times.

"Everybody sees the millions of dollars out there that I'm supposed to be turning my back on," Tiger said. "But what happens if I go pro and don't do well? I'll have no place to play. Where am I gonna go? Asia?"

But if Tiger harbored any lingering doubts about his future, golf legend Jack Nicklaus vanquished such apprehensions.

"There isn't a flaw in his golf or his makeup," Nicklaus said of Tiger. "He will win more majors than Arnold Palmer and me combined. Somebody is going to dust my records. It might as well be Tiger, because he's such a great kid."

So a new "Team Tiger" was beginning to emerge. I had been retained as a talent scout for International Management Group, the Cleveland-based firm that represents dozens of superstar athletes, while Tiger was playing junior golf; since I was seeing all sorts of junior golfers, they felt I was uniquely qualified to help them scout future professionals. And IMG eventually would take on Tiger as a client. Before he turned pro, we talked to professional consultants in every area of busi-

ness and athletic expertise, to guide us to make the right decision.

While Tiger still had every intention of finishing his college education and completing his degree—and that is still the
long-range plan—we all finally concurred that turning pro at
this point was the wisest decision he could make.

And so to alert the world that Tiger Woods would turn pro
in the fall of 1996, we decided to release a statement to the
media at the Greater Milwaukee Open, where he would play
late August that same year.

It read: "This is to confirm that, as of now, I am a professional golfer."

PART 3

• •

HELLO, WORLD!

Chapter Seven

• •

"TEAM TIGER"

Aт 1:36 P.M. on August 29th of the 1996 Labor Day weekend, Tiger Woods hit his first shot as a professional, as he teed off at the Brown Deer Golf Course in the Greater Milwaukee Open.

The national media descended on this milestone occasion like mice to cheese; television cameras, radio stations, sportswriters . . . they were all over the story of the 20-year-old kid who was about to take the PGA by storm.

But Tiger, the most heralded golfer to come out of the amateur ranks since Jack Nicklaus 35 years earlier, seemed unfazed by the hype. Behind the scenes, I could tell that Tiger was more relieved than nervous about turning pro. He had played a practice round with Dave Stockton Jr. and Billy Andrade at Brown Deer Park earlier that week and appeared happy and relaxed. Still, there was understandably a degree of tension as he prepared to tee off that first day.

When the atmosphere at tournaments gets really crazy and hectic and the crowds are closing in, as they were at that first pro event in Milwaukee, Tiger and I have a unique way of communicating on the course: We call each other using a secret code name. And as Tiger worked his way through the masses on his way to the first tee to hit his first drive as a pro, he heard a familiar voice calling out to him.

"Hey, so-and-so," I yelled out to him, catching his attention. "Just remember that I love you." The same loving reassurance I gave him when he was 6 years old at the Junior World in San Diego. I saw him smile, and any lingering tension just vaporized. Then he stepped to the tee and tore into his drive, 336 yards, right down the middle.

I knew he'd be okay. It was the beginning of a season that would be historic, thrilling, devastating, eye-opening and, above all else, unforgettable. It would be a lot to digest, but Tiger possesses an extraordinary quality that enables him to do extraordinary things: He has the poise to step up his performance to the next level of competition, analyze the situation and dominate like crazy. He never is intimidated or in awe of his competitors, not since that fateful day at the Junior World in San Diego when he was eleven years old. He loves a challenge. And so it was with his advancement to the PGA ranks.

After winning three U.S. Amateur titles, there was little else for Tiger to accomplish on the college or amateur level. Even his college coach, Wally Goodwin, extended his best wishes to his former pupil. "I jumped for joy," Goodwin said of the news. "He's ready. He's a great kid. He has paid his dues. He has been a wonderful emissary for Stanford the last two years." So the time was right for him to move on to the pros. No regrets, no looking back. Tiger was ready to tee it up for a new round in his life. Good-bye, NCAA! And good riddance!

But along with the excitement over Tiger's announcement that he was turning pro came many other opportunities and decisions that had to be handled responsibly. We decided that International Management Group (IMG) would act as his agent, with a team headed by Hughes Norton, who has handled many of the world's top golfers. We hired professional consultants and agents for Tiger's investments. People we trusted. We wanted everything done right; it was important to us that the world knew who Tiger really was, what he stood for.

Much has been made of the fact that before Tiger had even hit a ball as a professional, he was already a multimillionaire, thanks to enormous sponsorship contracts with Nike and Titleist. This is all true, and we think of those corporations as essential, integral parts of our team; they have been wonderful friends and business partners, and I am grateful for the role they have played in our plans, and their willingness to make a tremendous commitment to a young golfer who had yet to prove himself as a PGA professional.

But I feel I need to address what that money has meant— and what it has *not* meant—in our lives.

First and foremost, playing golf never has been about the money. The money is meaningless. Tiger could have three times the endorsement dollars if he moved like so many other young athletes: Get every quarter you can get and run. Notice we have no car endorsement; no soft drink endorsement; no fast-food endorsements. These are the three major "prizes," the product endorsements most young athletes hunger for. Not

Greg Nared, Nike tour representative, squires Tida around a tournament site.

that we haven't received many wonderful offers. We've also had tremendous foreign endorsement opportunities, but we've pursued very few. But we all wanted Tiger to be free to focus on golf, not on shooting commercials or making appearances. I'm sure there are those who cut corners and make promises that they probably can't keep, but we take Tiger's commitments very seriously. For example, Tiger and I spent three days of negotiations with Nike aimed at producing a Tiger Woods line of clothing. If Tiger's name is involved, we are personally involved, and we make sure everything is done right—first class, top quality all the way.

Tiger is one of the owners of the All-Star Cafe nationwide, but he has no interest in opening up a restaurant under his own name. In fact, for the whole area of licensed products— zero interest. It's too early, too time-consuming, too complicated . . . and Tiger doesn't need that at this juncture of his career. I am trying to keep it simple. Nothing is more important to me than his comfort and welfare, and he's just not ready for all of that.

From the beginning, I have made it my priority to always do the best thing for Tiger. I am trying to make sure that he is here for the long haul, rather than going for broke and burning out. I have been astounded by criticism and lies in the media that Tiger has been used and manipulated into taking on too much, that his game has been affected by other obligations and commitments. What an incredible misrepresentation of the truth. There is nobody in this world who has Tiger's best interests at heart more than his father, and he knows it. And I could care less what anybody else thinks. I don't have a hidden agenda. I don't live my life vicariously through him. I have had my day in the sun. I don't need to be in the sun anymore.

And so when Tiger began his first pro season, and many were saying he might be the greatest golfer who ever lived, I thought about what that really meant. Did I care whether he would be the greatest ever? Not as much as I want him to be a good person, a happy person. Tiger's success as a golfer is a means to having a platform on which to do good things in the world, not a means to promoting sandwiches. If that comes at some point, fine, but our priority is to let Tiger grow, mature and become the man he wants to be. Money doesn't motivate me, and money doesn't motivate Tiger. Tiger cannot be bought. Neither can I.

So while he was flattered and excited by the big endorsement deals, he never once felt like he "had it made." He has no comfort zone. If anything, the exorbitant contracts only intensified Tiger's resolve to perform at his best and give back to the people who were supporting him. Ask him which has more value to him: a multimillion endorsement check, or a much-smaller paycheck that he earned playing golf. No contest—the money he earns playing good golf is worth everything to him. That is what is important to him. The rest is like Monopoly money.

Honestly, if Tiger quit golf tomorrow and said he wanted to be a fireman, I would say, "It is going to take a little training, but I want you to be the best fireman you can be." And the rest would be up to him. Because if he wanted to quit, that would be sufficient for me. It is his life, not mine, and he is entitled to live it the way he wants to live it, without interference on my part. I try to be Tiger's mentor and adviser, and he makes the decisions. I provide input and information; the rest is up to him.

You might think that because we had traveled so far, spent so much time and exerted so much effort—the long road trips, the financial and personal sacrifices—that the economic windfall would send us all spinning. After all, our lives had changed radically and completely within the framework of a few whirlwind days. But the fact is, we were not totally overwhelmed by the sudden onset of riches and fame. I think it was a testament to our initial resolve to place principle and purpose above fame and fortune. Who we were remained more important than who we were about to become.

From the start we realized that we needed to create some policies and rules about how to handle the avalanche of offers and inquiries that were pouring in. And so we established a system based completely upon Tiger's welfare. What is good for Tiger? Our priority during the first year of his professional life was to get him adjusted to the PGA Tour and find out what he could and could not handle. Period. We had to be very care-ful about taking on endorsement responsibilities, which always translate into significant time requirements, because we were committed to staying focused on Tiger's primary goal to play well. We had to learn: How much would this affect his play? How much would it affect his rest? His mental attitude? His preparation?

We've established a committee of three people who vote on all endorsement opportunities. That committee consists of Tiger, his agent Hughes Norton and me. You notice there are three so that there can be no ties. And we all vote independently with our own conscience, always keeping in mind what is best for Tiger. Interestingly, every vote has been unanimous.

But I also have the sole authority to declare a moratorium on added endorsements or extra activities, and say enough is enough. And I am the only one who can lift the moratorium. This is not about having power over my son; it is about taking the heat, being the "bad guy," so that Tiger doesn't have to worry about any of it. I take the blame if we decide to turn down an opportunity or someone is about to be disappointed. Tiger focuses on golf.

I have declared two moratoriums, and have lifted one of them. The first one came after Tiger first turned pro and signed his initial endorsement contracts, what I consider his "core" contracts, with Nike and Titleist. Then the moratorium went into effect, and we focused only on golf and getting his pro career started without the distractions of having to think about business deals.

We had mentally divided the season into thirds, with the first third concluding after the Masters. At this point, we reevaluated his progress, his schedule and his whole demeanor. Based on his performance and how well he was handling himself, I lifted the moratorium to allow another round of endorsement contracts, including American Express, Rolex and a website at CBS Sportsline. And then I declared another moratorium, currently in effect, which I have no intention of lifting until it's absolutely in Tiger's best interest.

It has been a learning experience for all of us, including the "expert" among us, Tiger's agent Hughes Norton. My relationship with Hughes has been ongoing since I was a talent scout covering the American Junior Golf Association Tour, back when Tiger was 14 or 15 years old. Hughes is one of the top three guys in the International Management Group, and he has been the agent for many of the world's top golfers. However, Tiger presented a unique challenge, and Hughes immediately shared our vision of how to give Tiger the best shot at being successful, on and off the golf course.

But beyond his father and his agent, Tiger also needed to surround himself with other young people who could relate to what he was going through. Unfortunately, unlike other sports where rookies have teammates and coaches around them, Tiger was pretty much left alone by the other golfers, with the exception of a few. His closest friend on the Tour was—and still is— Mark O'Meara, who really took Tiger under his wing. He was pretty close with Woody Austin, too, until Woody's game went south and he lost his PGA Tour playing privileges. In general, though, it was a lonely existence out there for him. The only golfers even close to his age were 26, 27, 28 years old, and most of them were married. So Tiger didn't feel like he fit in; he couldn't socialize with them, didn't eat with them, didn't drink with them. And to compound the problem, there is a "caste system" on the PGA Tour, whereby "superstars" aren't likely to associate with rookies and journeymen players. They are never

Tiger and his agent Hughes Norton trade hats in a moment of levity outside Tiger's home in Orlando, Florida.

Butch Harmon gives a swing lesson to Tiger at Houston, Texas.

Tiger and Mark O'Meara compete on the putting green. Although friends, they are also deadly competitors.

paired with each other in the first and second rounds. Never. And to be sure, the other golfers at his own level did not seek him out. But the most paramount issue is that there are no other black golfers. No other Asian golfers. As it has been his entire life, Tiger is the only one. Since he was three years old, he has been the "only one." It is a lonely existence.

So he was fortunate to befriend other young, successful athletes from other sports, who really helped him with the transition to the PGA and into the international spotlight. Michael Jordan, Dee Brown, Penny Hardaway, Gabrielle Reese and Ken Griffey Jr. have all been good friends to Tiger. Tiger and Junior Griffey, his off-season neighbor in Orlando, Florida, are together all the time, playing golf. These friends are all older than Tiger, and many of them have been through something similar to what Tiger experienced as a newcomer. They gave him good advice and counsel. The best advice anyone gave him was, "Take this information, use it and then make up your own mind and do what you want to do."

Despite the explosion of interest in him, Tiger understood from the start that fame could be fleeting; the pitfall of being a big star is losing sight of who you are and what you want to accomplish. He watches his friend Michael Jordan, near the end of a glorious NBA career, make some great moves to keep his name in front of the public, because Michael knows fans can forget very quickly. Remember Bo Jackson? He was the biggest star Nike could have dreamed of—bigger than MJ at the time—but he became injured and faded fast from the marketing scene. You can be the biggest headliner in the world, and one day, the ride can be over. And what do you have left? Yourself. The person you were when you came to the party. If you can't put that into perspective, it will overwhelm you, and that is the danger of public life for any celebrity. That is why it is so important to me that Tiger understands who he is, that he likes and respects who he is. It's the only way I know to keep him from becoming overwhelmed by his new lifestyle.

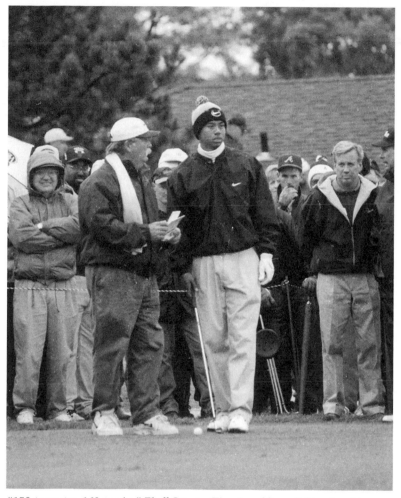

"150 to center, 162 to pin." Fluff Cowan, Tiger's caddie, reliably gives him correct yardage to execute the next shot.

Handling his status as an international celebrity never has been as big an issue with Tiger; he has been something of a celebrity since he was a little boy. But he looks at himself as a person who has to watch his p's and q's. He doesn't look at himself as somebody entitled to special privileges. He is aware of the inherent responsibilities that go with who he is. He also is aware of the pitfalls. It is not an easy task. It is often lonely. That's why he surrounds himself with friends and family—the people he trusts. That's his coping mechanism.

From the start, it was obvious that Tiger wasn't the only one benefiting from his entry into the professional ranks. The game itself seemed to receive a shot in the arm along with a financial windfall, increased popularity and heightened visibility, due in large part to his emergence. People who had never before watched the sport were tuning in to see how he was doing, and folks who had never been on a golf course in their lives were trekking out in all kinds of weather just to get a glimpse of him.

Tiger's new visibility also helped the PGA Tour substantially increase its overall rights fees in deals with CBS, NBC and ABC and cable's ESPN, USA and Fox Sportsnet: In the spring of 1997, the PGA announced that a new television package will dramatically increase tournament purses. The agreements, which begin in 1999, could almost double payouts by 2002, according to commissioner Tim Finchem. Where the average purse had been $1.7 million, Finchem estimated the average purse should go up to $3 million by 2000 and $3.5 million by 2002, the final year of the four-year package. The new TV deal also set up the long-awaited world tour, featuring three events in 1999. Besides the traditional World Series of Golf during the summer, there will be a world match-play event in February and a stroke-play tournament in November. And if you think that the networks might have gone a little crazy over the sudden popularity of a relative newcomer, consider this: An estimated 44 million people watched at least a portion of Tigers' final round in the Masters.

It was undeniable: As Tiger's first season began to unfold, the television ratings were skyrocketing. People couldn't get enough of the charismatic kid with the million-dollar smile. He was like watching lightning. There was sheer electricity when

Fluff Cowan "supervises" putting practice.

Tiger was on the course, and it even came across on that damn television. And people loved it. You never knew when this kid was going to go off and put on some spectacular display, like he did at Pebble Beach or the Masters in his first year. He just electrified the whole event.

Suddenly, people were coming to golf in droves. I was traveling all over the United States and everywhere I went, people were saying to me, "I had never been to a PGA tournament in my life. I never watch golf on television, because it is too boring. I watched Tiger once, and now I am hooked. I go to the golf tournaments. And in fact I am taking up golf myself. I am starting to play. . . ."

What is it that has reached out and grabbed them? God, I don't know, but there is something there. People seem to relate to his competitiveness, his spirit, his obvious enjoyment.

So many other professional golfers don't reflect the joy of the game. They look like they are bored to death or scared to death. Tiger just looks like he is having fun out there, displaying his emotions, letting it all show. I think that's what made basketball, especially professional basketball, so wildly popular in the '80s and '90s: The players were finally showing some emotion, and people could see that these kids enjoyed what they were doing. They were artists, they were creating. Tiger is the same way in his sport. He is bringing joy to golf, and sharing it with everyone.

This is a quality that I didn't give him. This is something that came from somewhere else. There is a glow that permeates the atmosphere when he is around, and I don't know what it is. But it sure does draw people to him, as if they've known him all their lives. I think the sport lends itself to a certain familiarity, since people play it themselves. Who do you relate to: a seven-foot basketball player or a 170-pound golfer who resembles your brother-in-law? Fans are able to identify with professional golfers much more than they identify with athletes in other sports. They've been right there on that course. They can't play it the same way, but with the handicap system, they can compete against these guys in an equitable fashion. There is no such thing as a handicap in basketball or football or baseball or track and field. Also, unlike other sports, golfers are out there in plain view, with no helmets, no uniforms, no protective gear, nothing. And golfers are closer in proximity to the crowd than they are in any other sport.

As Tiger began to march through his historic season, there

was no shortage of well-wishers and truly great people who supported Tiger. Unfortunately, there's a small group of sick people in our society who get their kicks making death threats against celebrities, and Tiger was not exempt from these. It was nothing new: Death threats against Tiger have been a recurrent theme throughout his career. There was no sudden increase in them when he turned pro; they had been there consistently over the preceding years. And so when he was thrust into a situation where throngs of fans were following him everywhere, in extremely close proximity, concerns over security measures increasingly crossed my mind. I am always concerned about his physical safety.

In years past, security for PGA events had been left to the discretion of the individual tournament directors. And, until Tiger joined the Tour, security did not seem to pose an overwhelming issue. But now the galleries had swollen to almost unmanageable proportions, and the sheer crush of people was frightening. Tiger didn't want to say anything, but I could tell that the lack of security in certain situations was getting to him. So I addressed the issue with PGA commissioner Tim Finchem, and now security measures on the PGA Tour have been improved dramatically, for *all* golfers. They now have a security consultant for the PGA Tour who goes around to each Tour stop in advance and briefs them on security measures and procedures. There are now standards that all Tour sites must comply with, very little of which existed before.

Tiger has always received hate mail, which he reads— every bit of it. And I approve of that; I don't want him to be surprised. I want him to know. I have never hidden anything from Tiger in his entire life. I have always talked to him and told him the truth. He always knows. And in this case, I feel to be forewarned is to be forearmed. Still, it isn't a pleasant experience, and despite the improvements at the tournament sites, everywhere else that Tiger goes presents an ongoing security nightmare; we are constantly reassessing what to do about those threats. Tiger had never had a bodyguard, but we are beginning to see the need for a security companion, someone to run interference for him and make sure he gets where he is going, safely. It is unfortunate, but it is a fact of life. Incidentally, all of Tiger's death threats have come from the United States, a sad commentary.

As the season got underway, we continued to make every conceivable effort to make Tiger's transition go as easily as possible, to keep his head clear and his shoulders free from the heavy burden of celebrity. Yet there was one other cloud hanging over his head; the one thing no one could control but me.

It was at the Tour Championship at Tulsa, Oklahoma, in October 1996, shortly after Tiger's pro debut, that I suffered a minor heart attack. I had already undergone quadruple bypass surgery in the mid-80s, so believe me, I knew what was happening. I was admitted to St. Francis Hospital in Tulsa early on a Friday and spent four days undergoing stabilization treatment, tests and observation for chest pains.

Looking back, I don't know whether it was the stress of worrying about Tiger's first year on the PGA Tour or my smoking habit that contributed more to my heart problems. Perhaps, it was a combination of factors. Whatever the cause, it was terribly hard on Tiger, and he found himself unable to focus on his game, which only brought me more stress. I knew I had to get control of the problem, for both of our sakes.

When I was stabilized, I returned home to California, where I met with my own cardiologist. After taking a variety of tests, I was given a choice of approaches. I could attempt the non-surgical approach, which entailed a dietary plan prescribed by the Scripps Clinic in San Diego, involving a severe dietary change accompanied by exercise and yoga. It would be far less invasive than surgery, but I felt the need to get at the problem as directly as possible. I chose the surgery.

And so in mid-February 1997, as my son was launching his first full year as a professional golfer, I was having surgery and a triple bypass procedure. I was in intensive care for three days. But as painful as it was for me, it was a nightmare for Tiger. At my insistence, he was trying to compete, and as I successfully recovered from the surgery, Tiger was staying in touch with me by cell phone from the golf course during the Nissan Open at Riviera Country Club. We had taken so many precautions to see to it that Tiger would be worry-free during his rookie year, and here was his dad, lying in intensive care. It was absurd.

Even more absurd were the bizarre pitfalls I fell into on the road to recovery. Thank God for my ability to hang tough, because I don't know how I would have survived otherwise. First, during recovery, I developed a strange case of the hiccups and was not permitted to have any water. The hiccups got worse and worse, triggering muscle spasms in my back. I told the hospital attendants: "Let me get out of this bed, because I am not going to die in this bed." So they finally agreed to let me sit down in a chair, with all of these tubes hanging out of me. I remember asking for a towel, which I put underneath my robe. I sat there shivering and shaking from muscle spasms and hiccups. I was miserable.

Meanwhile, I was tearing my whole insides out. Suddenly, I noticed there was a drip, drip, drip on my foot. I looked down and everything was coming out. I remember thinking: "Oh, God, we're in trouble!"

That's the last thing I remember. I am told I had emergency surgery to repair the damage I had caused with the hiccups. Afterward, the surgeon looked at me and said, "You're a real warrior."

I said, "Yeah, I have just been to the place where the ultimate competition is held, and I found out the competitor was me."

He looked at me and said, "And you won."

I said, "Yeah, I did. I wasn't supposed to come out of that."

To really complicate things, the doctors had decided during the emergency surgery to not completely close me up, because there was an area they didn't think would heal from the inside out without some help, and there was some fear of infection. So they left the damn thing open. For a full three-and-a-half months, I had to go around with this unclosed area on my chest, cleaning and dressing it night and day. I saw my doctor every day for three-and-a-half months, twice a day at the start. It was debilitating, difficult and very restricting for me. I was forced to watch my own son on TV because I couldn't be there for him, which was unthinkable. Still, I was always there in spirit, and he knew it.

I made it my goal to carry on as best I could to help Tiger in any way possible. I suppose my absence helped him to grow and learn more things on his own, from experience, which has always been my goal for him. I know I won't be here forever, and I want him to be completely self-sufficient when I'm gone. His first year on the Tour presented him with a multitude of opportunities—good and bad—to discover just how much there was to learn. The year seemed riddled with controversy, although very little of it was caused by Tiger. Still, there were one or two episodes I feel I could have prevented, had I been healthy and present.

In late November 1996, Tiger was widely criticized for his sudden withdrawal from the Buick Challenge. He was exhausted and worn out by his intense schedule as well as his concern for my health. So he withdrew from the event, which included an awards banquet where he was to receive the Fred Haskins Award for the top college golfer of 1995–96. The banquet was subsequently canceled, and a lot of people were very upset.

Tiger took a lot of heat for his decision, and I believe that if I had been involved, I could have saved him from himself. How? I would not have allowed him to go home. I would have allowed him to withdraw from the tournament, because he was mentally and physically exhausted. But I would have convinced him to attend the banquet, which was being held in his honor, and then go home.

I later talked with the officials from the Haskins Committee to find an agreeable way to resolve the situation. They came up with three recommendations: cancel the banquet, hold it at a site agreeable to Tiger, where there could be a presentation without a banquet, or reschedule the banquet at the same site.

I went back to get Tiger's reaction, and his immediate response was to reschedule the same banquet, in the same place. It would involve far more of a commitment than the other two choices, but, as he said, "I owe it to those people."

So he did it, and it was a smashing success.

I can be on top of Tiger. I can travel with him all the time. I can be there beside him advising him every step of the way. And I can prevent about 85 to 90 percent of the problems he encounters. But what happens when I am not there? He has no experience to fall back on. Like any parent, I want to preclude my young son from making painful mistakes. But I also want Tiger to grow and learn things on his own. My philosophy has been to separate myself from Tiger, allow him to muddle through and learn from his own mistakes, as distressing as they may be to watch.

If you are a parent, you know the discomfort of disciplining your child and thinking, "This is hurting me more than it is hurting you." If you are a child, you hear that and think, "Right. Sure."

But as an adult, you know it's true: It does hurt you more than it hurts them. And it does hurt me to see Tiger encounter public relations situations that I could have taken care of, just by being there. Yet I am willing to pay the price so that he can grow up to be his own man. It is going to pay dividends later, because his core is good, and he is a responsible individual. He will do the right thing. He may make mistakes, but he will end up doing the right thing in the long run, because his heart is in the right place. He doesn't know everything, and he doesn't know how to handle all situations. But he is a fast learner, and I am giving him the room to learn.

I never have been one to set goals for Tiger. That is because he sets his own, and his own are so high that they exceed my expectations and everyone else's, too. What I try to do is deal in reality. I know that Tiger is an ongoing painting, and the painting is far from complete. He needs me for years to come, and he counts on me being there for years to come. Whatever role or whatever needs I might fulfill for him, I will be there to do it for him. Tiger knows that. We are a team. That is where the term "Team Tiger" comes from for our organization. We still call ourselves a team. He says, "Pop, we make a tough team, don't we?" And I say, "Yes, we do."

So with our team—and our philosophies—firmly in place, we watched Tiger's historic season explode before the public eye. But all our careful planning and arranging couldn't have prepared us for the events that were about to unfold. The game of golf was about to be changed forever.

• •

Chapter Eight

THE ROOKIE

THE ADRENALINE WAS pumping faster than the blood from my heart.

Could that possibly be my son, walking down the 18th fairway at Augusta National? He walked as if he didn't even notice his feet touching the ground. I guess that's what someone looks like when they're on Cloud Nine. It was the most surrealistic, magnificent moment I have ever witnessed.

It was already a foregone conclusion that Tiger was about to win his first Masters tournament. Now it was simply a matter of how wide the margin of victory would be and how many records would be shattered along the way.

I recall that I was totally, physically exhausted; the heart surgery two months earlier had completely sapped me of energy, and I just didn't have it strength-wise. Yet I was so exhilarated. And, most importantly, I was alive.

Under any other circumstance, I should have been at home, recuperating. But I just had to be there in Augusta, if only to watch from the distance of the clubhouse. Tiger knew how seriously ill I was, and it was weighing on him mentally; it had become tough for him to focus. When his mind isn't clear, it is difficult for him to play. So I needed to be with him, just so he wouldn't worry about me, what my condition was, or how I was doing. He could see me every day, look me in the eye and know that I was OK and that he didn't have to worry about anything.

It had been my goal all along to make it to the Masters, to watch my son play there for the first time as a professional. So I took my doctor with me, and he monitored my condition and changed my dressings every day. I couldn't walk the course, but I was there. And I was there talking to Tiger every night about how he played that day and what the strategy would be the next day. Truth be told, we were sustaining each other with our presence.

It has been part of our tradition that Tiger and I meet on the 18th green after 72 holes. So I was determined to be there again on this momentous occasion, come hell or high water— or heart surgery. I arrived at the 18th just as Tiger was finishing up the 15th hole. Someone from CBS Sports said to me: "Mr. Woods, we have a television monitor over here where you can

Magnolia Lane, Augusta Golf Club, home of the Masters.

watch the tournament and sit down." He took me over by the TV tower near the putting green, and I rested while watching Tiger on the little screen.

And there I sat, staring at the screen in stunned amazement, my ailing heart pounding. As I saw him make a great putt on the 16th hole, I said to no one in particular: "Wow! He two-putted it from way on the right side of the green with about a 30-foot break." He had about a six-inch target in which he had to almost stop the ball, then allow it to change direction and trickle down the slope toward the hole. Too long, it picks up speed and goes off the green down the bank into the water. Too short, it takes a severe break and almost comes back to him. Amazing doesn't do it justice. It seemed unfair that anyone could possibly make that shot, but Tiger did.

Then I watched him at the 17th. By now it was clear Tiger would win, and members of the media began descending on the area around the final hole; suddenly everyone wanted to interview me. I talked to the writers briefly, excused myself and walked over to the 18th green, where Tida and I were positioned in front of the scoring tent. By then Tiger had teed off, and I kept waiting and waiting for him to show up near the green. I said to myself: "Oh, no, Tiger. You're not going to do something dramatic again on the 18th hole, are you?"

Sounding more like a giddy fan than a parent, I muttered aloud: "Where's Tiger?" Somebody answered: "He's way down the hill over on the left-hand side of the fairway." As if I had spotted an apparition, I exclaimed, "Oh, my gosh! That's Tiger!"

I saw this little white ball pop up out of a multitude of people—an absolute sea of human beings. The ball landed on the green.

"Well, that's Tiger, all right," I deadpanned.

And then, as if I was watching a dream, he emerged from the crowd, head high, right arm pumping in the air, smiling from ear-to-ear, acknowledging the thunderous cheers and chants from the gallery like a victorious politician.

It was sheer pandemonium, and for a frightening moment, I was really concerned for his safety. Tiger was stuck down there in that mob. Later, after I viewed the television tapes, I was horrified to realize that my concern was totally justified, because he had no security support at all as he headed to the fairway. He was even separated from his caddie. Tiger was lost in the mob, and lucky for us, it was a loving mob. One little kid darted right out of the masses, ran up to Tiger after he hit his shot and patted him on the back. At that point I thought: "Oh, God. Just for the grace of God, that could have been someone crazy."

But when Tiger broke free, I had instant relief from my anxiety. Now I was overwhelmed by an indescribable, awesome sense of pride. I thought, "This is his dream. I am watching him accomplish his dream!" It was beautiful to see as a parent. I didn't break down; I wasn't emotional at that point. I was simply observant.

Tiger walked up to the 18th green and acknowledged the crowd. I knew, however, that despite the commotion and excitement, he was still most concerned about sinking that final putt. And I was right. He was all business. He never lost his focus. He immediately went into his pre-putting routine—the routine he had performed so many times that it was automatic, no matter how critical the situation, no matter how great the stress—and forgot all about the crowds and other external distractions. He focused on this one putt, a very difficult, downhill, break-left putt—a double-breaking putt, to be exact. He ran it about four feet by the hole.

I said to myself: "There is no way he is going to miss this." Tiger just doesn't do things like that on the 18th green. Under adverse conditions, he just maintains his poise. He does things dramatically. He just raises his level of performance.

Sure enough, he drained it. Tiger had just won the Masters by a record 12 strokes.

First, Tiger shared a private moment with his caddie, Fluff Cowan.

Then, as Tiger came towards the scoring tent, he headed straight into my arms. That, of course, is when I broke down. I lost it. I just told him: "We did it! I love you! I am so proud of you!"

Tiger said, his head cradled on my neck, "We did it, Pop! We did it!"

And then we both broke down.

It has always been *"we* did it"—never *"I."*

I told Tiger, "Let it go. Let it go." When he was in my arms, he was safe; he was free to relax. That is our ritual. That is the closure for a tournament. Emotions release from both of us, and I realize, "God, I am participating in this."

I don't know how long we hugged. It didn't seem long; we were just in our own world. That hug, and the many that came before and after, is so beautiful, so simple, but so completing and fulfilling for both of us.

I guess after a while I let him go. And while he was hugging his mother, a tournament official was apprising me that there was a potential problem. Tiger had a situational ruling out on the course, and I wanted him to double-check with the officials before he signed his scorecard.

Tiger said, "No problem, Pop. It's all squared away."

I said, "Double-check anyway, before you sign your card."

So he double-checked, and there was indeed no problem. You just don't take chances like that.

Tiger later told the press, "What I think every time I hug my Mom or Pop after a tournament: It's over. I accomplished my goal. To share it with them is something special."

What an incredible thing to hear your child say.

For the record: Closing with a 69, Tiger finished at 18-under par, 270, the lowest score *ever* shot in the Masters. The score matched the most under par by anyone in any of the four Grand Slam events. His 12-stroke victory over his nearest competitor Tom Kite was not only a Masters record by three strokes, but the greatest winning margin in any major tournament since Tom Morris Sr. won the 1862 British Open by 13 strokes. He just went out and brought the course to its knees and beat it.

I will never forget the infectious smile on Tiger's face when he slipped his arms into the symbolic green jacket presented by defending Masters champion Nick Faldo. Tiger Woods, Masters champion! I liked the sound of that.

It seemed like television cameras were everywhere, but what they had not captured were the private late-night conversations Tiger and I enjoyed during the tournament.

The night before the final round, Tiger had gone out for a walk and then he came into my room. It was 1 o'clock in the morning. Tiger picked up my ice cream and started eating it. Then we talked about the next day.

I told him that his round the next day probably would be the most difficult round of his life. But if he could just be himself, I said, then it would be one of the most rewarding.

As we talked, I realized how important it had been that I made the trip to Augusta.

Tiger saw that I did what I had to do to be there for him in spite of my physical health. I don't use physical illness as an excuse or an explanation. You just do it. You just go. You find a way. If I could be tough, Tiger knew he could be, too. And this toughness has served him well.

The entire world had watched us embrace after the Masters. But there had been other similar moments between us, long before he had ever become a professional. For instance, when Tiger won his first U.S. Junior title, he was the first black man in the history of the United States ever to achieve this. And when he was in my arms and we were both crying, I told him: "Son, you are now a part of American history. You will always be a part of American history because of what you did today." Then we had yet another similar experience when he won his first U.S. Amateur title in such dramatic fashion.

With Tiger, everything is such an emotional roller-coaster. Ninety-nine percent of the time are highs for him, and you tend to have an unflappable faith in him, because you know he owns those last two or three holes of a tournament. Or he owns overtime. His willpower and his mental strength are so great that he just controls the whole situation. You expect these good things to happen. And, quite frankly, they do. It is beautiful to watch. His mental strength is improving all of the time. I notice it when I have been separated from Tiger for a month or so. When I see him again, I can tell he's tougher in some way; it's like watching ice harden.

I just hope that Tiger doesn't toughen himself up so much that he loses touch with his real emotions. Now, there is a fine line there. That's why it is so important that we have this emotional release at the end of tournaments. The embraces represent the human, emotional side of him coming out. It is critical that Tiger has this escape valve.

Such expressions of a partnership between Tiger and me are manifested in . . . I won't say higher standards of performance . . . but a mental tenacity, which far exceeds that of a normal person. It's almost as if he has the power of two. Because Tiger feeds off me. He always has.

While Tida tends to be more emotional during Tiger's tournaments, I try to remain unflappable and comfortable with the whole situation, regardless of how things are going. I do this for Tiger, because when Tiger sees me there, very cool, very calm, under very traumatic circumstances, he gains strength from me. There are times when he's playing poorly, and he looks over toward me on the sideline, and he sees me laughing. I mean no disrespect to him at all, and he knows that. But it's my way of saying: "Hey, son. It's a game. And quite frankly, you're not that good." Tiger will just shake his head, thinking: "I'm struggling my tail off, and Pop's over there laughing." But he understands it's a game, and I hope he never loses sight of that.

All of the excitement surrounding Tiger's Masters victory almost made me forget my health problems. But my post-surgical health still had to be addressed.

Prior to the Masters, while I was convincing my doctors that I was well enough to go to Augusta, I made an agreement with them that if the proper healing did not take place after my operation, I would have another surgery to correct the problem. When I returned from Augusta, the doctors took a look at me and said they were going to have to operate.

So they made a 6-inch incision and began to hack away at the old tissue, in order to get nice new tissue. I ended up with a two-inch wide, three-and-a-half-inch deep trench in my stomach, right below the sternum. That's how much meat they took out. Then they began to suture it together. Then they stapled it. For the first time in about four or five months, my body was finally closed up, and it started to heal. That's when I realized I was on my way back, but it has been a slow, steady process. Since then, I have taken my treadmill test, which verifies the effectiveness of the bypasses, because the tests jack-up my heart rate. I passed that with flying colors. That cleared me for physical training. I have hired a personal trainer, who inflicts as much torture on me as I do on her.

Unfortunately, while I was struggling last year to rebuild my strength and recover from yet another operation, Tiger was beginning to struggle as well, which was distressing but nonetheless a part of the game. He is harder on himself than anyone else could ever be, and so when he made some remarks that he was not playing his "A" game, even though he won some tournaments, he caught some early flak. Other golfers interpreted his comments as disrespectful, as if he was saying, "Hey, I just won the Masters by 12 strokes, and I'm not even playing that well!" But that was in no way what his comments meant.

Tiger's remarks were in no way intended to be disrespect-ful of the other golfers. What he meant was this: When you are at the top of your game, that is your "A" game. And anything less than that is, well, less. If you are at about 80 to 85 percent of your top game, then that is your "B" game. When nothing is working, then you are down to your "D" game. It is a way of evaluating your performance. It has been done since golf was first played.

Jack Nicklaus used to grade himself all the time, although he didn't use the same terminology. He would say: "My putter isn't working" or "I'm not hitting my irons crisp" or "I am not hitting my woods straight." These were indicators that he was playing at the "B" or "C" level.

The truth is, if Tiger is on his "A" game, nobody is going to beat him. I don't care what you have—his "A" game beats yours any day. Now, if Tiger is on his "B" game, there are a lot of other golfers who can beat him with their "A" game. And if Tiger is having his "C" game, he can still win a tournament, but he has to do it by impeccably and imaginatively managing himself around a golf course. And if somebody else doesn't have their "A" game, Tiger can still win.

Tiger learned that from conversations with Nicklaus. Nicklaus flat out told Tiger: "I very seldom won with my 'A' game. I won with my 'B' game and my 'C' game and I managed."

He said: "You have the same thing."

I have seen Tiger start off with his "A" game, and it is awesome to watch. In the Pacific Northwest Amateur when he was sixteen he was playing the 36-hole championship final round. Tiger recruited me to be his caddie. His opponent shot 1-under par that morning for 18 holes. He was 8 holes down because Tiger shot 9 under par. Then in the afternoon round, Tiger got another caddie, because I refused to caddie for him anymore. It's an in-joke between us. He walks so fast with those long legs that I'm forever trying to catch up. It lends itself for some very caustic ribbing between us. Believe me, he can insert the "needle" very good—so can I! Tiger proceeded to shoot an eagle and two more birdies and closed the guy out 11–10 for the championship. That was Tiger's "A" game.

I also saw Tiger at the Pac 10 Championships during his sophomore year at Stanford, when he broke the Pac–10 scoring record that had been held by Corey Pavin. Tiger had a 61 and a 65 that day. That's what he does when he has his "A" game.

The key to Tiger's game is his mental state of mind. When his mind is clear of other problems, and he is free to think of nothing but golf, then he brings out his most powerful weapon: his creative mind. That is when he is free to play, and it is beautiful to watch. He becomes like a machine. A beautiful machine purring along. Perfectly in tune. It is nothing physical or mechanical. It is all mental.

After the glory of the Masters, people started humming that he could win the Grand Slam—that is, win the Masters, U.S. Open, British Open and PGA Tournament in the same year. At some point, I don't think that is out of the question for Tiger. And breaking the record low score of 59 for a competitive round is definitely attainable by him. But last year, it wasn't to be, nor did I expect it.

Tiger's list of accomplishments at the midway point of 1997 included three consecutive U.S. Junior Amateur championships, three consecutive U.S. Amateur championships and four PGA victories, including the Masters, in only 16 tournaments as a pro. At 21, Tiger was the youngest to win a major since Gene Sarazen won the U.S. Open and the PGA Championship at 20 in 1922. And with such an auspicious start, even the once seemingly impossible mark of 20 career major championships by Jack Nicklaus seems attainable.

But Tiger would have many learning experiences last year, along with some stinging losses. I look at those experiences as part of his education as a professional golfer. For sure, some of Tiger's most profound lessons in maturity were realized through non-winning efforts.

For instance, Tiger thought he was going to win the PGA

Championships in Mamaronek, New York. When he realized he couldn't win it, by virtue of him playing with an injured ankle, he said to himself, "OK, that's all right."

You see, when Tiger is in the hunt to win a tournament in the last round, you don't see him laughing and talking with Fluff Cowan, his caddie, in the fairway. But near the end of the PGA Tournament, there he was, laughing and talking with Fluff. It was his attempt to keep his spirits up. He was disappointed that he didn't win, but at the same time, he understood: You can't triumph every time. The winner of this one, Davis Love III, just played very well.

Then in late August, Tiger had entered the Canadian Open at the last minute, and he missed the cut for the first time in his pro career. I had recommended against him entering so late. I wanted him to go home, get off his sore ankle and rest up. We agreed that he would go home and get treatment on it. Then,

The scoreboard reflects that Tiger is leading the Las Vegas Invitational. He went on to win his first tournament as a pro by defeating Davis Love III in a playoff.

Tiger plays a practice round at the British Open at Royal Lythan. He finds the British bunkers pretty deep and difficult to get out of.

Tiger hits a shot from the rough at the British Open.

Inside the ropes at the British Open. Tiger prepares to hit his approach shot to the 18th green during a practice round with Tom Kite, Davis Love III and Justin Leonard.

Tiger and Davis Love III pose with security guards after finishing a practice round at the British Open.

The presentation ceremony on the 18th green after Tiger won the 1997 Byron Nelson Tournament in Dallas, Texas.

based upon how it responded, Tiger was to give me a call and let me know which way he was going. He really wanted to go up there to play in Canada, he said, so off he went.

Unfortunately, he bit off more than he could chew. He was physically and mentally exhausted, and he needed rest. Not only for the ankle, but for his head and the rest of his body as well.

His performance showed it: Tiger started his day with a triple bogey and ended it with three bogeys on the last four holes. He shot a 76 and finished at 146, one stroke above the figure needed to qualify for the weekend rounds.

Up to that moment, Tiger had made the cut in all 25 PGA Tour events since turning pro, as well as in the 1996 British Open as an amateur and three international events going back to his missed cut in the 1996 Scottish Open, when he was still an amateur. Yet he tried to be philosophical about it.

My son and granddaughter, Tiger and Cheyenne, have a moment to themselves while he was competing in the Phoenix Open in 1997.

My granddaughter Cheyenne visits with her grandfather during the 1997 Phoenix Open.

Tiger said, "It had to happen. I can't play my entire career without missing a cut."

In retrospect, he admitted to me that he had made a mistake in judgment. It's very unusual for Tiger to miscalculate his own capacity, but he did. So he went home after the Canadian Open and said, "I am going to be a couch potato and rest up."

Which is what he should have done before the Canadian Open. We were all learning.

Tiger's final triumph of the season had come a month earlier, in July, at the Western Open in Lemont, Illinois. Following poor finishes at the Memorial, the U.S. Open and the Buick Classic, he had spent a week fishing, and now, refreshed from a week away from golf, Tiger had been ready to play.

He began the final day of that tournament in a three-way tie for the lead (with Steve Lowery and Justin Leonard), but three birdies over a four-hole stretch on the back nine helped him claim his fourth victory of the year. He shot a 4-under-par 68 for a four-round total of a 13-under 275 that was three shots better than Frank Nobilo of New Zealand.

In a season full of triumphs and disappointments, perhaps the lowest point was the Ryder Cup, played in October 1997. My original feeling about the Ryder Cup was that it would be a warm and glorious experience, watching my son represent his country abroad in international competition. The Ryder Cup was being played in Spain at Valderrama, so on his way to the British Open, Tiger made a stopover in Spain to play that course, just to see how it felt. That was when I had my first inkling that we were in trouble.

Tiger reported to me that by virtue of the design, the golf course effectively took his driver out of his hand and reduced him to a journeyman professional. The nearest parallel I can make would be going into combat with a pistol to fight an enemy who is equipped with a rifle, machine gun and artillery. He was very disillusioned by the course and felt it was poorly contrived, poorly designed and gave an unfair advantage to short hitting golfers.

On top of that, the European team had the advantage in course knowledge because their Tour Championship had been held at Valderrama; they were totally familiar with the nuances of the greens, as well as the configuration of the course. So I knew the American team was in deep trouble. No matter who we sent over there, they had to play out of their minds in order to win. If they merely played well, they would lose. If they played great, they might still lose. If they played outstanding, they just might win. That's how much the deck was stacked against them.

I had every intention of going to the Ryder Cup, until approximately three weeks before the tournament. I had waited and waited and waited for an invitation from the PGA to go along with the team. None came. Then I talked to Hughes Norton, who had just returned from Spain.

He said, "Earl, you really don't want to go, unless you are a member of the official party. To start off with, the nearest hotel is 40 miles from the golf course. There is one two-lane road from the city to the golf course. Under the best conditions, it takes 45 minutes to get there. But during the week of the Ryder Cup, they are estimating that it will take anywhere from three-and-a-half to four hours to commute to the course."

Then he said, "When you get there, what are you going to do? You will have 30,000 people to fight. Not only will you be fighting for position to see Tiger, but you'll be signing autographs right and left all over the place, because there is no place for you to go. No security, no nothing.

"Finally, there will be only four groups out on the golf course at one time. Many of the people will be following Tiger's group. So the chances of you seeing Tiger are slim and almost none."

Well, I thought, I just want to be present for Tiger, to be available, even if I'm not at the course. I said, "Well, when Tiger finishes, we can talk in the evening."

But Hughes informed me, "Actually, every evening is tied up with team meetings, team social functions and activities, which you can't attend unless you're part of the official party. And then you face this three-hour commute back to your hotel, where you sit all alone at night, not being able to talk to your son all day or all night. What's the point?"

So, based on this information, I made two decisions. One, I wasn't going to go. Why subject myself to that misery? And, second, I determined that I would make my non-presence a form of protest against the PGA for their decision to allow only wives and girlfriends to accompany the players as part of the "official party." There was no provision for parents or others to be officially sanctioned. Let me point out here that Tiger wasn't the only one affected by this: The policy was equally unfair to Justin Leonard, the only other bachelor on the team, as well as Brad Faxon, whose wife had notified him a week before the

Ryder Cup that she was seeking a divorce. Why should they too be forced to travel alone?

Still, I have to ask whether it was a conscious decision designed to exclude me specifically and deprive Tiger of his support system. Clearly, it was no secret early in the season that Tiger was going to make the Ryder Cup team; he was the No. 1 point-getter early in the summer. It is also no secret that Tiger is single, and certainly common knowledge that Tiger's support group is his father and mother. It is well known that I travel with Tiger, and share a suite with him whenever possible. Sometimes we barely cross paths, but he likes knowing I'm next door, I'm there for him. I have spent many, many, many days, weeks and dollars traveling with Tiger to tournaments his entire life, to ensure that I would be there when he needed me. Now, at Tiger's moment of greatest need while representing his country, I would not be there as he wanted.

Officials from the PGA Tour now insist there was no conscious intent on their part to slight or discriminate against Tiger and me by not inviting me to be a part of the official entourage that flew to Spain. In fact, I had a conversation with Jim Awtrey, current chief executive officer of the PGA, about this matter at the start of the 1998 season. Wives or girlfriends traditionally have been the only ones invited to accompany Ryder Cup players. PGA officials claim they were not aware any problem existed until they were airborne on the Concorde and disparaging quotes from me were read in *USA Today* onboard. After Tiger arrived in Spain, he told their local reporters the policy that kept me at home in the United States should be revisited.

The team consisted of captain Tom Kite, Fred Couples, Brad Faxon, Jim Furyk, Scott Hoch, Lee Janzen, Tom Lehman, Justin Leonard, Davis Love III, Jeff Maggert, Phil Mickelson, Mark O'Meara and Tiger Woods. They departed for Spain via the Concorde, along with wives, girlfriends and officials. And, of course, the sportswriters. Obviously, I wasn't aboard. Nor were the caddies of the players. It seems that the caddies weren't welcome in the official party, either.

On the third day after he arrived in Spain, I got a call from Tiger. He said, "Pop, I'm having problems with my putting. I am tired. I am fighting sleep deprivation. I have been so busy that I don't even have time to take a nap."

We talked for a while, and then he said, "I have to try to get myself some sleep tonight; I'm playing 36 holes tomorrow." That was the opening day.

I heard how tired he was, how exhausted he sounded. What I missed was his unspoken message to me: *Pop, I need you. I am having trouble with my putting, and I trust no one with my putting except you.*

This is how Tiger talks to me. He doesn't always directly say what he wants to communicate; he speaks to me indirectly, and I can almost always tell when he's getting at something else, and I pull it out of him. But this time, I didn't get the message.

Well, as the record will reflect, he did have putting problems. And that affected his game all the way back through his irons and his short game. He couldn't make good use of his driver, so he was floundering. Effectively take away a driver and a putter from any golfer, and see how well he plays. The course had rendered his driver useless, his putting was off, and as a result of the PGA policy, Tiger was all alone. In addition to that, the required post-golf activities were so great that the golfers had no time to rest. Of course, this affected all the golfers, not just Tiger, but most of the others had companions, supporters. Tiger was a 21-year-old, 10,000 miles from home, with no one to talk to. Alone.

That was the handicap that Tiger was under while he was at Valderrama.

Under the circumstances, Tiger did the best he could. He fought and he fought hard. But you can't shoot your enemy with a pistol when they have rifles. And Tiger quickly found that out. So after spending Friday and Saturday getting his brains beat in, he realized, "I have to have help."

So he desperately called me on the telephone. He called my house, and I was not home. I was playing golf. Tiger called his mother and she tried to get in touch with me, leaving a message at the golf course. When I finished playing, I called her immediately and I found out what the crisis was. We tried to call Tiger in Spain, but by then it was late afternoon Saturday in California, and late night in Spain. We figured out the time differential and figured out we should call at about 9 P.M., California time. But when Tida called the number that Tiger had given her at his hotel, she was told by the switchboard that he had a "Do Not Disturb" on his phone and they weren't able to ring the room. Of course, we really didn't want to wake him if he was finally getting some much-needed rest. So we found out that the Ryder Cup team would leave for the golf course the next morning at about 9 A.M. their time, which meant that we had to call at about 11 P.M., our time, which we did. But we didn't realize that Tiger was teeing off in the third group, and he had already left for the course by the time we called.

So frustrating, so unnecessary. To be a parent and not to be able to reach out to a child in need, to not be able to do for Tiger what I had always been there to do . . . it was upsetting beyond belief. Tiger has always come to me for help with his putting, and in this instance, when he really needed it, I wasn't able to help. And the tragedy of it all was that I could see on television exactly what he was doing wrong.

As the record reflects, Tiger did not play well, and the U.S. lost. He took home just 1½ points from five matches. As one of the three major title winners on the team (the others were Justin Leonard and Davis Love) many people blamed him for the Americans' 14½–13½ defeat to the Europeans.

Tiger's failure to cope with the tight, tree-lined Valderrama course underlined what had become apparent in the three other majors after the Masters: His game at this point is more suited to wide-open courses such as Augusta. Believe me, we are working diligently to correct this.

Several days after returning home to the United States, Tiger called me and said he was trying to rest up and get his energy and strength back for the last three tournaments of the season. I asked him, "Did you enjoy yourself in Spain?"

Tiger said, "You know me, Pop. I enjoy myself whenever I play golf."

I said, "Did you play well?"

"No, I did not," he said.

"Did you need me?" I asked.

And Tiger said, "Yes, I did."

And I apologized to Tiger for not being there when he needed me. It was the first time in his life that I have ever apologized to him for not being there when he needed me. Because it was the first time in his life that I wasn't there. And it hurt. And it still does.

I don't place full blame on the PGA and its policies. Part of the responsibility was mine. I was the one who made a conscious decision not to go, in view of the obstacles and the problems that I would face not being a member of the official party. Yes, it would have been easier for Tiger to contact me if I was 40 miles away, compared to 10,000 miles away. But hindsight is perfect.

And out of the clear blue sky, Tiger says, "By the way, Pop, what was it that I was doing wrong with my putting?"

I said, "You were doing this, and you weren't allowing that to happen, therefore it caused you to pull each and every putt."

And Tiger said, "Yes! That's it. No wonder I was pulling every putt. God, I wish I had known."

And I said, "I do, too."

So the Ryder Cup was a major disappointment for the Woods family. It was a learning and growing experience for Tiger, and he will never forget it. And he will be a better person as a result of it. But he didn't have to go through that alone. I recommend strongly to the PGA that they immediately review their policy on who can accompany the members of the team. I recommend that each member of the team be authorized to have one support person with him to accompany him, regardless of who it is. The choice should be the player's. All players should have the same rights and privileges. That is what my public protest was about—what is fair and what is just.

I have taken considerable personal flak from the media—especially from the Golf Channel—for the position I took, and I do not appreciate it. And I do not think that I was treated fairly. I received only one call from anyone in the media asking about my decision to boycott the Ryder Cup, from a member of the Associated Press. The call went like this: "Mr. Woods? Are you Earl Woods, the father of Tiger Woods?"

"Yes," I said, "Who is this?"

"This is So-and-So from the Associated Press. And I am calling to get your reaction to the story that broke in an English newspaper about you not being able to go as a member of the official party with the American Ryder Cup team. What is your position?"

I explained to him exactly what my position was. And his retort was: "Do you feel that this whole thing is racially motivated?"

And I said, "Hell, no."

His reply: "This isn't the kind of story I'm looking for. Thank you for your time." And he hung up on me.

So, in summary, I had one inquiry from the press. And what an inquiry it was. But despite being criticized relentlessly from all corners, do you think this will stop me? No, because I know that I am right. And I have the courage of my own convictions. My conscience is clear. Equal rights, equal privileges.

After the Ryder Cup, a lot of blame was placed on Tiger for playing poorly, although I don't think it was an inordinate amount of blame. It was just frustrating, because we felt his poor play could have been prevented.

Shortly after the Ryder Cup loss, Greg Norman decided to be openly critical of Tiger, in particular for his sub-par performance. Why he felt this was appropriate, I do not know.

"Tiger", said Norman, "is proving to be a lot like everybody else on the PGA Tour.

"Tiger got off to a phenomenal fast start," Norman said. "But he's come back to reality, and he's just another golfer out there, like all of us, who's going to have his ups and downs."

Norman was speaking from his Florida home in a prerecorded interview played at the announcement of The Players Championship at his home course of Royal Queensland in December 1997.

"In any profession when there's a lot of hype, the individuals that play the game understand that," Norman said. "And in a career like golf, it takes decades to really smooth itself out and see how good you are over a period of time."

Norman went on to say: "The hype has put [Tiger] up on a level, and now, the way his play is, it's not up to that level and the hype has calmed down."

Now, remember Tiger twice took the top spot in the world rankings from Norman in 1997 before falling back to his final ranking at number 2. And as I write this, he is number 1 again.

I have a few things to say to Mr. Norman.

Where was Greg Norman when *he* was 21 years old? What had he accomplished or won when he was 21 years old, in comparison with Tiger? What was his record his first year on the tour? I will take Tiger's record up to this date, over Greg Norman's any day. Because I know that Tiger is going to get better.

I don't think that I am being overly defensive, bitter or nasty: I just call it the way I see it.

When it comes to Tiger's relationship with the other golfers on the Tour, I think the Ryder Cup afforded him an excellent opportunity for the other players to get beyond his game face, to get to know Tiger personally. Tiger is a prankster, humorous and easy to get along with. There is no aura of superstardom or spoiled brat about him. The Ryder Cup offers golfers the rare opportunity to play on a team, and I am hopeful that the others got to know Tiger better and will spread the word about what he is really like: easy-going, fun, competitive, and a great guy.

No doubt, Tiger's late-season troubles "humanized" him in the eyes of the others, although, believe me, he was pretty human to begin with. He is not a superhero. He is not a cartoon hero. He is a young man, with hopes and dreams and the right to make mistakes just like everyone else.

What went wrong for Tiger late in the 1997 season? Aside from being tired, there were some common mechanical problems he encountered. Yes, even Tiger experiences mechanical problems.

Tiger has a tendency to get the club closed at the top of his backswing, and he also has a habit of bringing his arms in toward his body. His hips are so fast and they rotate so quickly that his arms get stuck behind his body. They don't get out in front, and they don't keep up with his hips, and he can't have a smooth release through the hitting area. So his club comes in open, and he has to flip his hands to control the ball flight. I have seen him accomplish miraculous shots doing that. But this is what his swing coach, Butch Harmon, has worked on with him. In fact, in his initial session with Butch, after Tiger had been eliminated from the U.S. Amateur in Houston, I watched as Butch had him hit some balls on the driving range.

Butch said, "Tiger, you know, Greg Norman has a great pair of hands. But you have the greatest pair of hands I have ever seen in my life."

Now he had Tiger's attention.

And Butch told Tiger: "Therein lies your problem. I will bet that you can sense that when you come into the hitting area that your club face is slightly open, and that you manipulate your hands a little bit to square your club face up. Or if it is slightly closed, you hang on a little bit to square the club face up. Don't you?"

Tiger said, "Yeah, I do that, all the time."

So Butch said, "What we are going to do is get your swing so that as your clubhead comes into the hitting area in a square position more repetitively, it will free you up with your hands to work the ball."

It made sense to Tiger, and he bought into the whole program. He knew what his flaw was. He knew he got stuck and had to flip his hands through to control the club face. Butch got on it right from the start. He isolated the problem. He identified it, and he told him what he planned to do about it. And that was the making of a partnership. That's when I walked away from them, went over to a chair under a tree, sat down and watched them from a distance.

Tiger already had a mental checklist regarding his golf game. But the checklist has gotten longer, and his swing has become more repetitive and standardized. A classic example of that was in his most recent Masters tournament in 1997. After nine holes, he was four over par 40 and had played absolutely horribly. He analyzed his swing, identified what he was doing wrong, made the proper correction and then went out and shot six-under par on the back nine.

I have always insisted that Tiger's instructors teach him not only what to do, but why he should do it so that he could make adjustments on his own on the golf course. Thus he began developing this checklist. As he went from level to level and one teacher to the other—he has only had three teachers, not including me—that checklist list grew and grew. When he is in trouble and his swing isn't working properly, he will go through this checklist. Then, bang, out pops this solution, because he has been given the tools.

As far as his swing was concerned at the end of his first season, Tiger was hitting the driver better than he ever has in his life. He hit the driver well in the Las Vegas Open, and he hit it well at the Tour Championship in Houston. That was the one thing that stood out. He had finally mastered the driver. When Tiger was a little boy, I told him: "Don't worry about using the driver, because you are too young."

Tiger would say, "Well, other boys are using the driver."

I replied, "That's OK. They're bigger than you. And when you get old enough, we will put the driver in your bag. The driver is going to be the last club that you will master." And it was.

Another mitigating factor in Tiger's late-season decline in 1997 was the fact that he used his clubs so much that they were worn. Especially his 8-iron and his sand wedge. He did not want to replace them in mid-season, because he didn't want a "bastard" club in his bag. Fortunately, when Tiger hosted his first Tiger Woods Invitational in Japan last November, he was given his first new set of Titleist clubs. And, of course, Tiger endorses Titleist products. Those new clubs were a thing of beauty. I picked up his wedge, and it was balanced so beautifully. All of the clubs are just gorgeous.

The maturing of Tiger during his first pro year, his ability to handle the good times and the bad, turned everything around. The players on the PGA Tour began to appreciate him better and understand him better. Even the sportswriters began to say they noticed a major change. In Houston during the Tour Championships, I overheard one writer say to another: "You know, look at Tiger, he is so poised and so comfortable. He has really grown in this one year. And it is all positive."

The 1997 experience for Tiger represented a time in which he won more than he had ever won before, but he also lost more than he had ever lost in the past. It was an adjustment of sorts. Tiger is a realist, and he knows he is not going to win like he did at the previous level. He understands it is going to take a little more time before he can do things like that. I have cautioned Tiger that he is not physically mature and grown yet. It is going to take a little time.

In planning for the 1998 season, we had to go back to 1997 and study Tiger's results. It was the year we devoted to letting Tiger get established as a Tour professional and made several committed efforts to allow that to happen in a way that would make him comfortable. For example, the first thing that we learned was that Tiger could not handle four tournaments in a row. So we reduced it to three, maximum. Then we found out he could not handle five tournaments in six weeks. That's too much. And the big thing that we learned in 1997 was that Tiger would have to learn to pace himself better, so he would have more strength and stamina. You see, he's not physically ready yet.

In examining Tiger's 1998 schedule, you very rarely will see him play more than three weeks in a row. He probably will take two weeks off between matches, and he may take three weeks off. This is not going to be a popular decision, especially for the PGA, the networks and the tournament officials. There is enormous pressure put on Tiger to participate in every major tournament, and understandably so. He is a viable financial and economic weapon. When he is there, he has a major impact on that tournament, and their attendance and their financial success. When he is on the television screen, there is an electricity at the tournament that is not there when he isn't.

But our primary consideration is Tiger's welfare. I don't care what the tournament officials may say. If Tiger could make everyone happy by playing in every PGA event, he'd never have time to sit down. During the first 10 months of 1997, the longest stretch of time that Tiger spent at his home in Orlando was 10 days. We have no animosity toward any one Tour stop, and we hope no one takes these decisions personally. But it is more important for Tiger to develop as a viable pro on the PGA Tour than it is for him to be the most exhausted golfer in America. I know there will be flak. I know there will be pressure. I know there will be unhappy people. But we have to do what is best for him. It isn't so much a matter of Tiger being selective about in which tournaments he participates; it is a matter of him choosing to take his rest. Pacing himself. That is the thing that has to be conveyed to the tournaments. It has nothing to do with them. It all has to do with Tiger. So if two events came up on consecutive weeks and the Bob Hope Classic was the second of the two, well, Tiger wouldn't play in the Bob Hope. If the second event was Pebble Beach, he wouldn't play at Pebble Beach. It has nothing to do with that tournament. It is all about pacing.

By the end of the 1997 season, there was only one thing left for him to do: win the Tour money championship, or the Vardon Trophy. Now, the Vardon Trophy is based on a golfer's performance on average. By that point, it was pretty hard for Tiger to influence his chances based on total performance, because of the way the scoring is done. Player of the Year standings are based on a point system using tournament wins, official money standings and scoring average. The four majors are worth 30 points each, with the World Series of Golf and The Players Championship worth 20 apiece and the rest of the tour events worth ten points. Tom Lehman, the 1996 British Open champion, won the award in 1996.

Since most of the tournaments were completed, his chance for the Vardon Trophy was to become the leading money winner. And that is exactly what he tried to do. We didn't schedule or enter into any more tournaments to increase the chances of that happening, but it was a rallying cry for him that he could focus on to get through the last grueling weeks of the season. The opportunity to end the season as the leading money winner was really high on his priority list; he really wanted it. Not because the money was so important, but because in the sport of golf it's one of the few ways to measure your success. And after the disappointing second half of the season, Tiger was hell-bent on showing just how successful he had really been.

There were only two players who had a chance of catching Tiger for the money crown. Davis Love III was one of them,

Superstars must learn how to sleep anywhere. Tiger catches up on some well-earned rest aboard the airplane.

and Justin Leonard was the other. And on the final day of the Tour Championships in Houston, Tiger was pretty disappointed because when he finished his round, the leaders of the tournament were just turning to the back nine, and it really looked as if Love was going to go on and win it.

If Tiger had finished in the top 10 that day, he would have won the money crown on his own. But by finishing tied for 12th, he needed a little help.

Tiger was pretty down about it, and before the leaders were finished for the day, he left the course to go back to the hotel and pack. In retrospect, if he had asked me what to do, I would have told him to stay and publicly congratulate Davis Love for achieving what he did. But he was so disappointed that he just left.

Since Tiger had already gone, I, too, left the course, while the leaders had about four holes to play. I, too, thought that

Davis Love was going to win. And by the time I got back to the hotel, I knew I had missed the conclusion of the event, along with any television commentary or any recap or analysis. But as soon as I got to my room, the phones started ringing. It was Hughes Norton calling from Cleveland, where he had watched the whole thing unfold. And he had to tell me what we missed: Tiger had won the money title. We were astounded.

I said, "That lucky little guy. He never does anything the easy way."

Tiger's first-half performance had earned him the U.S. Tour's Player of the Year award: He had won more than $2 million, setting the all-time PGA money earnings record. Every penny he earned after that was a new record. He missed out on being the *first* golfer ever to win $2 million in a single year, when Hale Irwin beat him to the punch by doing so on the Senior Tour, but the final numbers gave Tiger the overall record. I doubt that record will stand very long, since the purses are going to increase dramatically over the next two or three years. Still, he did it, in only his first year on the Tour, and that is something that no one can ever take away from him.

Shortly after the announcement came, I got a call from the Nike Tour representative that sometimes travels with and provides support for Tiger while he is on the road. He said, "The party is on in Tiger's room in 10 minutes, because Tiger has to leave to catch his airplane and we only have 45 minutes to celebrate."

So we all went to his room, where Tiger was holding court with this big smile on his face. He came into my arms and he hugged me. I said, "Don't you ever do anything the easy way?"

Tiger said, "You know me."

We ordered champagne, and I offered a toast to Tiger: "This is to your first year, Tiger, and to the kind of person that you are. This is to the next great golfer."

And the next great golfer celebrated his first year on the tour . . . with champagne and a cheeseburger and French fries. What else?

. . . .

Chapter Nine

THE "LOOK" AND THE ISSUE OF RACE

THERE IS A survival technique that blacks have developed over generations in order to successfully co-exist in a hostile environment in which obstacles are placed in their path, and where every element is completely intended to keep them from succeeding. We have learned to smile and perform. We've learned to laugh in public and to cry in private. It is painful. African-Americans all over know what I'm talking about.

But Tiger has been taught about that, too. He knows all about "The Look." We used to go into the country clubs, and "The Look" says: "What the hell are you doing here?"

I can remember going with Tiger to an all-male country club outside of Chicago, when he was the current U.S. Junior champion. And as soon as we stepped in there, the conversation stopped, like somebody had yanked down the venetian blinds. Everything stopped and did not resume until we sat down. And then it buzzed.

Tiger said to me, "You feel it, Dad?"

I said, "Of course, I feel it."

At that time, Tiger was the Junior champion two years in a row, which no one in the history of the United States had ever done. And unknown to the club members sitting around us, Tiger had indeed been invited there to play a round of golf with a member—we weren't looking for employment.

From that icy greeting, Tiger went out to play golf, and the word quickly circulated as to who he was. The next thing we knew was that we had a mob coming out to watch him. It went from "What the hell are you doing here?" to "Let's go out and watch Tiger Woods."

That's why the Nike commercial is so accurate when it says, "There are places where I am not permitted to play." If he had not been Tiger Woods, he would have been greeted with a silent "You don't belong here." And it might not have been so silent. (I have yet to meet a non-white who didn't understand and agree with what Nike said.)

But as soon as they find out he's Tiger Woods, it becomes a totally different thing. He was a celebrity. And that somehow made it okay for him to be there.

"The Look" is something every black person in America can feel, but most whites are oblivious to it, until it's pointed out. For example, Tiger's agent, the wonderful and talented Hughes Norton of IMG, is one of the top agents in the world. He has plenty of experience representing top golfers. He represented Greg Norman when Norman was No. 1, so he knows what it is like to be the agent for the No. 1 golfer in the world. What he didn't know was what it was like to be the agent for the first *non-white* No. 1 golfer in the world. He had no clue. It has been on-the-job training for him handling the controversies and uproars. You see, he never ran into these problems to the same degree when he handled Greg Norman, because Greg Norman is white. So he runs into these situations with Tiger, and there is no clear explanation. He says, "Why? Why is this happening?"

And I just tell him, "Hughes, don't you understand? Tiger isn't white."

And Hughes says, "Oh, I never thought of it that way. I see

what you mean now. I can see it now." So it is an ongoing educational process for him. But he is getting there. See, all of these
instincts that blacks have built up and developed through the
centuries have been survival techniques. We blacks take them
for granted. Hughes is getting in touch with them for the first
time. He didn't know what the hell we were talking about
when Tiger and I spoke of "The Look." He subsequently has
learned. Now he sees it firsthand on his own.

Tiger has been heralded as a groundbreaker, a trailblazer
for minorities in sports, and that is true to a degree. But he was
by no means the first. Jackie Robinson broke the color barrier in
major league baseball three decades before Tiger was born.
And Tiger was only a baby when Lee Elder became the first
black player to compete in the Masters in 1975. Tiger was 15
when Ron Townsend became the first black member at
Augusta National Golf Club in 1991. Four years later, Tiger
became only the fourth black competitor at the Masters, following Elder, Calvin Peete in 1980 and Jim Thorpe in 1982. The
best finish by a black player had been Peete's tie for 11th in
1986, before Tiger's triumph in 1997.

Jackie Robinson also faced discrimination on the golf
course, when he was denied membership at a private club near
his home in Stamford, Connecticut. He began playing golf in the
1940s, when his partners included Joe Louis and Charlie Sifford,
who won the 1967 Greater Hartford Open. That was only five
years after the Caucasian-only clause was eliminated from PGA
Tour membership rules. Pete Brown won the Waco Open in 1964
to become the first black champion in a tour event, but he wasn't
invited to the Masters. In 1970, Brown won the San Diego Open,
but again wasn't invited to the Masters. And even though past
Masters champions were allowed two invitees, Brown received
only two of the four votes required for entry, from Bob Goalby
and Art Wall. In 1972, Masters officials changed eligibility rules
to include all tour winners from the previous year. I guess you
can call that progress.

Tiger always has had respect for the black pioneers who paved the way for him to have an opportunity. "Obviously, Jackie Robinson is one of my heroes," Tiger told the media during the Masters tournament. "He has definitely inspired me. He did something that's just absolutely remarkable. . . . All the people who were against him doing something he loved to do was unfortunately a sign of the times. But if it wasn't for him, I don't know if other players such as Lee Elder or even Charlie [Sifford] would have done the things they did, because I don't know if they would have stuck through it without lashing out. . . . Jackie was the one who paved the way for all pioneers who are minorities."

Ironically, Tiger's record-breaking Masters performance came in the same year that major league baseball celebrated the 50th anniversary of Robinson's breaking baseball's color barrier.

To appreciate Tiger's current niche in the American sports framework, people need a refresher course on the recent history of racism in the world of golf. In 1990, the PGA of America came under intense criticism for awarding a major tournament to Shoal Creek, a private country club in Birmingham, Alabama, that practiced exclusion: no blacks allowed.

In a weak attempt to defend its decision, Jim Awtrey, the executive director of the PGA, said at a news conference: "Those courses selected for the PGA Championship beginning in 1995 will have minorities, including women and blacks, as members. Right now we are having conversations with the clubs hosting the Championship from '91 to '94. We will continue to have those conversations until such time as we've completed that analysis." In other words, it will take us five years to acknowledge what everyone else knows right now: that it's wrong to exclude anyone because of their race.

Well, if the PGA thought its weak attempt at political correctness would make everyone content, it was wrong. No one was buying it—particularly the sponsors. IBM was the first to declare that they would not advertise on the PGA Championship telecasts.

"When we learned that this tournament was being played at a club that was exclusionary, we decided it was not an appropriate vehicle for our advertising," said an IBM spokeswoman. "Supporting even indirectly activities which are exclusionary is against IBM's practices and policies," she said.

Then Toyota and Anheuser-Busch joined IBM in canceling plans to run television ads during the PGA Championship.

The cancellation of TV ads by major corporations came just as Birmingham's black mayor, Richard Arrington, took the role of racial peacemaker in hopes of convincing Shoal Creek to open itself to black members, avoiding protests and making clear to the rest of the country that Birmingham had become racially progressive in the past two decades.

Arrington said he had received a letter from Shoal Creek officials, which convinced him that the club soon would accept black members.

"It's a positive step," he said.

Meanwhile, a local black leader who had called for a picket of the country club said he believed the protests could be averted if the club would accept Mayor Arrington as a member. But Hall Thompson, the founder of Shoal Creek, said the club wouldn't be pressured into accepting blacks. He later apologized and said he was quoted out of context. Shoal Creek officials added that the club didn't have any policy against blacks and that some have actually been there as guests.

Now remember, this was in 1990, not 1890. This was just a few short years ago, when a survey by the Associated Press discovered that on the list of private country clubs hosting major championships that year, none had a black member. The controversy was now spilling over into other tournaments, as the membership practices of other clubs hosting PGA tournaments were being called into question.

The Shoal Creek uproar would not go away. The Southern

Christian Leadership Conference said it would picket the tournament if the club had no black member. In response, Shoal Creek admitted a black businessman as an honorary member and said it was processing another black for full membership. The Southern Christian Leadership Conference called off its plans to picket.

"We were very confident that Shoal Creek would reach that decision," said Jim Awtrey of the PGA. "I would say it makes a significant statement, because in a short period of time here it did indicate Shoal Creek's willingness to integrate the club."

Shortly thereafter, the PGA's board of directors approved its new site selection policies at a news conference. One clause in the policy stated: "The PGA requires that prospective host courses which are clubs rather than public facilities have demonstrably open membership policies and practices prohibiting discrimination on the basis of race, creed, color, national origin or gender, and that the maintenance of such open membership policies be contractually guaranteed."

Awtrey added: "Certainly we may be remiss in not addressing this in the past, but we think that the steps that we have taken now are very positive. They reflect positively on the game."

And, he said, the major championships hosted by the PGA were being held "at courses that do not have discrimination. We think that is a very positive step."

And that is how the PGA began requiring minority membership for country clubs conducting the PGA Championship, although none of the changes were required until 1995.

Of course, as Tiger is quick to point out, he doesn't only represent black golfers; he represents Asians as well.

While playing in a tournament in the Philippines in January of '98, Tiger said, "Asian golfers have the talent to win big tournaments in the future."

"It would be great for the game," Tiger said during a

press conference. "I would like to see more minorities win a major. . . . Unfortunately, traditionally they haven't had a chance. Now that the game has changed and doors are open, the opportunity is there. It's just a matter of time before you start seeing more minorities winning big tournaments."

Tiger knows he is in a unique position to inspire other minorities to *believe* that they can get somewhere, even when the rest of the world is telling them they can't.

"A lot of kids look up to me just because they can relate to me. I think that's the impact I would love to leave. One day when I am done with golf . . . we can all look back and say, 'You know what, Tiger made a difference in kids' lives.'"

But with change comes controversy, and with controversy often comes hatred. Despite the throngs of fans and supporters, there are still people in this country who do not want to see a minority succeed, and they are not afraid to let us know about it. We get our share of hate mail, which, as I wrote earlier, Tiger reads. He needs to know what is out there.

As part of his training, I introduced Tiger to Hank Aaron, when they were both at the Arete Awards for Courage dinner in Chicago. I told Hank about the hate mail, and he said, "He needs to know." And when Hank and Tiger had a personal talk, Hank told him about all of the hate mail he had received when he was chasing Babe Ruth's home run record. And how he kept them, and how he wants his grandchildren and children to know what he went through.

Hank told Tiger: "You are going to receive that kind of mail, too. You are not immune. Because you are going to be doing something in a sport that none of us have ever done anything in. And you are going to be more unique than I was."

I have tried to do the best I could to prepare Tiger for this, and basically give him the tools to help him watch his own back. He knows the truth: When it comes to the acceptance of minorities in America, our country still has a long way to go.

Sadly, there has been no real change since Shoal Creek,

despite the new policies and promises. Country clubs are paying lip service to black participation in their clubs, letting in one or two minorities, so they can say they "complied" with the rules. It's scary, but country clubs contain the power sources for every community in which they exist. They contain the banker, the mayor, the police chief, the fire chief, the businessmen, everyone who controls the community. And they are not about to permit a black to come in and be privy to all of that; it would upset the apple cart. We might be on the inside knowing what was going on. There is no shortage of qualified blacks for club membership in the United States; there's just a shortage of clubs that they have an opportunity to join. The clubs are not willing to give up that power. They run golf, and they run the United States. It's all about power and economic and financial opportunity, as well as political opportunity. They are not about to give this up.

It's north and it's south and it's east and it's west. And I see no chance for it to change in the immediate future. Tiger and I will do our part to try to effect change. We have what we call "quiet dignity." Tiger will handle everything with quiet dignity. There will be no problems. Whatever he does, he will do it with class. Now, there will be people who will not like that. And they may be resentful of the fact that he is behaving with quiet dignity. But do you know something? There is nothing they can do about it.

Whatever racial tension may have existed when Tiger burst into the pro ranks, it all came exploding to the surface, courtesy of fellow PGA pro Fuzzy Zoeller.

Zoeller made his now-infamous remarks regarding fried chicken and collard greens when talking about the next Masters dinner that is hosted by the defending Masters champion, who will, of course, be Tiger.

During a brief interview on CNN, Zoeller said, "That little boy is, uh, driving well and he's putting well. He's doing everything it takes to win. So you know what you guys do when he gets in here? Pat him on the back, say congratulations, enjoy it, and tell him not to serve fried chicken next year. Got it?"

As he was walking away, Zoeller turned to add, "Or collard greens or whatever the hell they serve."

Fuzzy Zoeller had built his reputation as one of golf's top ambassadors through a decade of outstanding efforts and personality. All it took was that one ignorant, uncultured remark to tear it all down. He lost years of goodwill, his sponsorship from Kmart, and he lost the respect of a lot of people.

My initial reaction was: "Maybe Fuzzy ought to go to Kmart and buy some common sense."

Responding to the firestorm over the comments, Zoeller said, "I was merely making reference to the Championship Dinner. In fact, when I hosted the dinner, I served fast-food hamburgers. I have nothing but the utmost respect for Tiger as a person and an athlete." He later said in a prepared statement to *Pro Golf Weekly*, "It's too bad that something said in jest is turned into something it's not, but I didn't mean anything by it, and I'm sorry if it offended anybody. If Tiger is offended by it, I'll apologize to him, too."

I was surprised at the intensity of the reaction to Zoeller's remarks, and I believe the remarks were meant as a joke. I think the story took on a life of its own. Tiger and I both felt that he should accept the apology and move on to bigger things.

I'm not surprised that he said it. Fuzzy is a jokester. But I was shocked that he said it publicly. It was a remark you'd expect to hear in a private conversation.

So I would like to get this straightened out once and for all. In the first place, Tiger had nothing to do with it. If there was ever an example of a victim being charged with the crime, it was Tiger. When the news first broke—the story didn't come out for almost a week after it happened—we were on a very important business trip to Nike, literally locked up in meetings all day long. At night we were so exhausted we just went to bed. The next morning, bright and early, we were up again and went directly into another all-day negotiating session. We didn't hear about the Fuzzy Zoeller thing for about three days. It may sound impossible, but we were so focused on our talks with Nike that we shut everything else out.

When Tiger finally found out, he was very shocked. And he did nothing about it, because he hadn't done anything wrong. We finished our meetings, and Tiger went up to Washington to meet up with his friend Kevin Costner, on location for a movie. And again Tiger was out of touch.

A couple of days later I am at home and Tiger calls me. He says, "Pop, this thing is breaking loose, and the players are starting to blame me. I haven't done anything!"

Tiger said, "We've got to do something about this."

I said, "OK, cool it. I will get back to you." I called his agent, Hughes Norton, and Hughes and I discussed what was going on. We decided that Tiger needed to release a press statement. And that's what he did, and that was it, because there was no culpability on Tiger's part. I thought he handled it very well, as a gentleman. In a statement issued through his public relations firm, Tiger said, "At first, I was shocked to hear that Fuzzy Zoeller had made these unfortunate remarks. His attempt at humor was out of bounds, and I was disappointed by it. But having played golf with Fuzzy, I know he is a jokester; and I have concluded that no personal animosity toward me was intended. I respect Fuzzy as a golfer and as a person and for the many good things he has done for others throughout his career. I know he feels badly about his remarks. We all make mistakes, and it is time to move on. I accept Fuzzy's apology and hope everyone can now put this behind us."

Incredibly, a couple of days later, Fuzzy made another ridiculous remark, which I won't repeat. I guess he didn't have time to get to Kmart for the common sense. And again the players were all over Tiger for taking so long to make a statement and not letting Fuzzy off the hook. People were saying,

"Why did Tiger let Fuzzy dangle for so long?" Well, Fuzzy dangled only because Tiger didn't know a damn thing about the uproar until well after it had exploded. And Tiger didn't do anything wrong. He didn't make a statement because it wasn't required. Tiger only did it because he thought it would stop the firestorm. To this day, I don't know whether the players' reacted so negatively toward Tiger because they were not informed, or because their prejudices were showing.

Now, if Tiger had made the statement about Fuzzy Zoeller. . . . Let's suppose that and imagine whether the other players would have defended Tiger the way they defended Fuzzy. I don't think so, at least not at that time. At this point, I think they would. Now that's progress.

The other golfers on Tour treated Tiger differently after the incident. There *is* lingering resentment on the PGA Tour. And it is totally unwarranted and unjustified.

In many ways, I have been disappointed by the lack of support Tiger has received so far from veteran golfers, particularly the black golfers, as few of them as there are. Incredibly, Calvin Peete made a statement during a television segment about Tiger not thinking of himself as black. Everyone has the right to his opinion, but Calvin Peete had never met Tiger when he said that, so he doesn't really know anything about him. And he has never, ever, helped Tiger in any way, shape, form or fashion. He has never talked to him, never called him, never offered anything that might assist him in his development. So I was astounded to hear him speak as if he was Tiger's mentor, as if he had tried to take him under his wing.

Calvin Peete has never heard Tiger deny being black; Tiger knows exactly who he is. Tiger says, "I am a black golfer, and I am also an Asian-American golfer." On the TV interview, Peete said that Tiger can't make up his mind what he wants to be. Well, it isn't a matter of choice: He is who he is. I feel sorry for someone who is so misinformed that he totally misrepresents the truth. Get with the program, Calvin.

I really don't concern myself with Calvin's motivation for saying those things. Whatever experiences he has had, he has never done anything for Tiger, and I have little respect for him. It is truly sad.

Other black golfers have criticized Tiger for not thinking of himself as a black golfer. Well, they are living in the 1940s—that's where their mind-sets are. This is the '90s, and people can be who they are, and be proud of it. The days of being ashamed that you are black and white, or black and whatever, are over. Today, people take pride in their multicultural backgrounds, as they should. It is their right. No longer does a child have to deny the existence of his mother or father just because they are of different races. The chromosomes are there. The genes are there. This is a day to celebrate who you are, not to be ashamed of your heritage. If Tiger has unintentionally become a role model for other kids of biracial backgrounds or multicultural backgrounds, I applaud it. *Be* the person you are. *Accept* people just as they are. *Life will work.*

For some reason, a great deal of energy has been spent by various ethnic groups insistent on claiming Tiger for their own. For the record, Tiger has responded by saying that he is a combination of several nationalities, including African-American, Asian, Caucasian and Native American, an answer that upsets all ethnic groups, each unwilling to share him. I say Tiger is a member of the "human race."

The week after the Masters victory, Tiger and I appeared on Oprah Winfrey's show, which was a real honor for us; ironically, the date had been set long before the Masters—it just turned out to be great timing. As usual, the subject of Tiger's race came up, and Tiger responded by saying that when he was younger, he had coined the phrase "Caublinasian": some of this and some of that, all blended into one. Well, there were a lot of messages delivered on that show, messages delivered to the whole world loud and clear, especially to the blacks who demand that Tiger pronounce himself as African-American, period. The message was this: *If I am not black enough for you, that's your problem. Because under no circumstances is the black community ever going to make me deny the existence of my mother. I am proud of who I am. I am proud of my father's African-American background. And I am proud of my mother's Asian background. And I am also proud to be an American.*

Well, that topic—combined with the uproar over the Fuzzy Zoeller story, which had just emerged—engendered such a strong reaction that Oprah did a follow-up segment the next week on the topic of Tiger's race. And despite those fanatics who ridiculously insisted that one drop of black blood makes you black, the general consensus seemed to be: Why must he choose? Why label him? And whose concern is it? Tiger is what he is, and he's entirely proud of his heritage, which is all that matters. I do not believe it is cause for international debate.

Frankly, with all the important and compelling issues surrounding today's stereotyped black athlete, I can't believe the time and attention that has been paid to Tiger's gene pool. Surely there are more pressing and significant problems to solve. For example, the outcry over the fact that there are so few positive black role models in sports, the growing perception that all athletes are bums and criminals, and the fact that the sports pages read like police blotters. No question that Tiger has emerged at a time when people, especially black people, are seeking someone wholesome and positive, someone to be proud of, someone to cheer for—reassurance that we are good people. That is why so many people find Tiger refreshing; he's like a breath of fresh air. Tiger's purity, his philanthropic attitude, his graciousness, poise and character are manifested in all that he does. And those are the exact things that this country needs right now. Not just this country, but the whole world, where Tiger's multiethnic heritage has connected him to both Eastern and Western cultures.

Even when Tiger was growing up, he understood that black or white, Asian or Indian, everyone deserves a fair chance. He watched his parents respect each other's heritage, and he watched us interact with many close friends, black and white. Four of my very good friends and golfing buddies, Roger Wells, Bob Rogers, Skip Habblitz and Bill Stark, are white, and they were great role models for Tiger. They are good people who made a distinct impression on Tiger and his development as a person. These friends reinforced to Tiger what my mother taught me: Do not judge people by their color. Tiger has no bitterness today toward white people because of these lessons and our openness to experiences with people of all colors. Those were important and essential early lessons for a black kid to learn.

Tiger has no agenda at all, other than to help and to care for people. I am the same way. All I want to do is the best I can to affect people positively. I am not saying we are saints; we certainly aren't. But we put our money where our mouth is. We are out there; we are doing things. Others are welcome.

The criticism that Tiger receives from other African-Americans does not surprise me at all. I am not bitter about it. I fully understand it, because it is politically motivated and it comes from the highest echelons of black leadership. It is all about power and political representation. If Tiger, one of the most popular figures in America, is not defining himself as strictly African-American, then he is supposedly subtracting himself from that power base, weakening that community. And as a result, he is viewed as strengthening some other political base, which is "multiethnic."

I imagine that every political group would love to have Tiger on board, but I do not see Tiger ever becoming involved in the political arena. Tiger is not a political person. He is a social person. Don't get me wrong: He will have political ramifications, I feel, because his fame and popularity will give him power. The power to do good; the power to help; the power to build golf into the most popular sport in the world.

Tiger knows that he has the potential to be one of the great ambassadors of golf, not just for minorities, but for everyone. As he has said: "I don't want to be the best *black* golfer. I want to be the best golfer." That was his way of saying, *I am good for golf. I am not just good for black golf. I am* for *golf; I am not just good for black participation in golf. Or Asian participation."* And he has put his money where his mouth is. He is proving it by his actions. Remember his "illegal" dinner with Arnold Palmer when he was still at Stanford? Tiger asked Arnold to dinner so he could hear about Arnold's experiences as an ambassador of golf, so that Tiger could prepare himself and be better able to function in that capacity and do the right things for golf. Tiger is a dreamer, but he is also very thorough and very prepared. Golf does not have to worry about Tiger leading it astray. He has too much respect for the game and for the people who have contributed so much to its development and popularity. He is just going to take this sport to another level that it has never known before, despite the flak and responsibility that goes along with this reality.

I see Tiger's role in golf over the next 20 years as similar to that of the first minority President of the United States. Tiger is going to be expected to do things that nobody before him was expected to do in that capacity. And he is going to be held to a much higher standard than others before him, like Arnold or Jack Nicklaus. The public and media never went into Arnold Palmer's private life.

There is no doubt in my mind that there are people in the staunchly entrenched, conservative element of golf's highest echelons who would stop at nothing to prevent Tiger from achieving his goals. I know they are there. I am watching them. You know how intuitively you know that there is somebody pushing against you? You know it. And one of these days I am going to identify those people trying to impede his progress and I am going to expose them. I have encountered this resistance throughout Tiger's development, and it comes from the highest echelons, where change is not necessarily considered a good thing.

But change is coming, and it will start with the kids. Just think about it, all of these little Tiger fanatics growing up in prejudiced, bigoted homes, for the first time starting to question or refusing to listen to the stuff spewed out by mom and dad about white superiority. Kids will say, "You're wrong." And all of these open-minded little converts will someday be in positions of influence, and that's when you are going to have change.

Kids can learn so much about life from the game of golf. They understand about fairness, equality, freedom, honesty, integrity, patience, understanding. They learn how to communicate and to respect other people's opinions. They learn how to play by the rules. The powerful groundswell is going to come from these children who are learning, at a very early age, that Tiger is the real thing. He is pure. You can't fool kids; they just know when you are lying or telling the truth, and when somebody is a phony and when they are for real. And they know Tiger is for real.

Our dream is that all of these kids who are looking to Tiger as a hero and a role model will grow up and spread the message into their communities, into their own lives. These kids are going to be in political office; they are going to be in the military; they are going to be police officers. They are going to be every place, all grounded in the lessons of life they learned through golf: respect, fairness, patience, understanding. Not only is golf going to get bigger, but the sociological ramifications of its teachings are going to get bigger and bigger. And the impact is going to get bigger and bigger.

Think about it: The mayor of the city is a golfer who wa an admirer of Tiger's when he was a little boy. Maybe th police chief was also a fan, and the banker, the lawyer, th judge and the list goes on. . . . What do you think is going to b the impact in that community? Think about it. What is th going to do for society? And Tiger is going to be here for a lor time, constantly putting positive messages out front for ever

one to see. And guess what? Every year there will be new children who will adopt Tiger as their hero and role model and go through the same process. By the time Tiger is on the Senior Tour, these children will have become parents, and they, too, can teach what they know. The possibilities are overwhelming.

Tiger is deeply committed to kids, so committed in fact that he passed up the opportunity to play golf with President Clinton because he had a date with some inner-city children.

While we were at the U.S. Open, there was an invitation for us to go to the White House, but Tiger had a higher priority: the kids of New York City. He had a clinic to perform on Monday for inner-city kids on Randall's Island. That was more important to him.

Accepting the responsibility as a role model is a task with which Tiger is comfortable. And being a role model for the black, Asian and white communities is meaningful to him, as well. He has also thought a lot about his multiethnicity and the resulting tug-of-war between his two cultures to make him their own. We have discussed how he is not black enough for a lot of people, and he is not Asian enough for a lot of other people. We explored and discussed these issues quite openly for years. That he has a whole race on his back now is not a surprise to him. He has known and considered this possibility for a long time. We always have come to the conclusion that: "You are you. And it is all right to be you. And if these people do not understand that, it is their loss and their problem. It is not yours."

Tiger's upbringing included a thorough indoctrination as to who preceded him on the pioneering trail of professional sports. Too many of our young athletes today lack that keen perspective, and frankly, it is embarrassing. What so many young athletes today don't have is a foundation of pride and self-respect. If they don't get it as children, they don't get it at all. Along with that comes a lack of appreciation for the contri-

butions made by their predecessors, whether in sports or government or science. For instance, I am appalled at the fact that professional baseball players do not know the story of Larry Doby, the first African-American baseball player in the American League. If you have no thread to the past, you have no ladder to the future.

None of these important details were overlooked when Tiger was growing up. I made sure that he knew his sports background. I put him in touch with the past. When he received an award at the Amateur Athletic Union Sullivan Awards in Indianapolis, I took the time to take Tiger by a golf course in that city, which was the only one that blacks could play on there in the early years. Hanging on the walls were photos of former heavyweight champion Joe Louis and black golfing pioneers Teddy Rhodes and Charlie Sifford. All of those guys had played there because that was the only place they could play. Tiger was just awestruck by the historical significance of this place. I asked the golf pro there to make a copy of one of the photos of Teddy Rhodes to give to Tiger, which he did.

Tiger was so impressed and so touched by this that he put on an impromptu golf clinic for the underprivileged kids in Indianapolis, right there in the rain. He was hitting golf balls out there while the rain was coming down, and the kids were just oooohing and ahhhing. There was a standing-room-only audience in the clubhouse. Tiger was having a ball himself. He was totally motivated, giving something back. It was a touch of history, and it was beautiful to watch.

To understand Tiger is to know that he comes from a deep sense of self-worth. He likes who he is. He respects who he is. And he does not need this validated from an external source or by materialistic wealth. He is very content with who he is. So, with his self-respect firmly in place, he is able to handle all of these issues. There are no insecurities at work. That's why he is so tough in the stretch run of a golf tournament. There are no questions; there are only answers. When he steps on the accelerator, the heart is what responds, because there is a tremendous heart there to be called upon.

Chapter Ten

EYE ON THE TIGER

LIFE IN THE MEDIA SPOTLIGHT can be both exhilarating and exasperating—a blessing and a curse. Just ask so many of our world's celebrities and dignitaries who have been scorched by

CBS Sports commentator Jim Hill interviews Tiger at Navy Golf Course in Cypress, California, while I listen attentively.

probing eyes intent on denigrating reputations and exposing private lives.

Don't get me wrong. There is a rightful place for the media as our public conscience. But a better, more thorough and professional job needs to be done when it comes to establishing the line between the right of the people to know and the basic human rights of the celebrities being virtually stalked by cameras and microphones day and night.

The media has its ever-present eye on Tiger, trying to scope out anything in his personal life that it can serve up as a sumptuous appetizer for a gossip-hungry nation.

For instance, in the summer of 1997, Tiger met and became friends with Sarah Ferguson, the Duchess of York. I don't call her "Fergie" like the British and American media do; I call her Sarah. It turned out that she and Tiger had some mutual friends, and she soon became a friend of our entire family. We first met her in Dallas at the Byron Nelson Tournament in 1997, and we instantly bonded and became friends. At the same

Sarah Ferguson, the Duchess of York, Tida and I take a break for a cool drink after watching Tiger win the 1997 Byron Nelson Tournament.

time, Sarah became infatuated with the game of golf and was completely hooked on the sport My wife loaned her a hat so that Sarah, who is very fair, wouldn't burn in that Texas sun. She had a great time at the tournament, and we all enjoyed her company. The press had a field day with her presence on the 18th green for the awards ceremony.

When Tiger traveled to the British Open in July of his first full season on Tour, the original plan was for Sarah to come to the tournament and we could all spend time together at the house Tiger had rented in Scotland. We later decided, however, that this plan would not work because Sarah is too big a celebrity there; her presence at our rented house would have brought too much unwanted attention. After all, the primary objective for our being in Scotland was for Tiger to play in the British Open, and we didn't want anything to get in the way of that. The last thing we needed was a circus like atmosphere surrounding Tiger (we had enough of that without adding any other distractions), so we didn't follow through on the plans.

Instead, Tiger and a group of his friends who were his guests at the tournament (whom I jokingly refer to as "The Rat Pack") decided to head over to the Mediterranean for a few days of R&R. So they all flew down on a plane for a week's vacation, just to hang out, have fun, each to enjoy a good vacation. Tiger had earned some time off, and he deserved it. Coincidentally, Sarah herself happened to be vacationing in the Mediterranean as well, so she and Tiger took the opportunity to meet up and spend some time together.

Well, he had a great time. The thing that amazed him was that he was able to sit down at a streetside cafe, have dinner and not be besieged by hundreds of autograph-seekers. Tiger said, "I couldn't believe it." That doesn't happen often worldwide.

But while the general population didn't bother him, there was a certain faction of the media—the group I refer to as the professional "snoops"—who were intent on spying on Tiger.

Tiger and the "rat pack" celebrate his 22nd birthday in Las Vegas.

Tiger takes a moment away from the tournament grind to "hang" with buddy Jerry Chang.

Wherever he went, there they were, just trying to catch him doing something outlandish. Sorry, but there was nothing to catch. So he had himself a good time while the snoops just waited and watched, all for naught, and it serves them right.

Finally, when they realized they couldn't find anything wrong or juicy in his conduct, they invented something. One tried to suggest an affair between Tiger and Sarah, but there was absolutely no substance to that report; just names and glitz. There was nothing newsworthy at all, not that that would be anybody else's business anyway. But the media was all over them, infringing on their personal lives by trying to breathe some life into a story that just didn't exist. Believe me, there is nothing between Tiger and Sarah, other than a great friendship.

Should he have tried to "hide" the fact that he was vacationing at the same locale as the Duchess of York? Are you kidding? Tiger is the type of person who cherishes friendships very highly. It never enters his mind that others might perceive a relationship as something other than what it really is. He knows what is truth, and what is not, and that's all he cares about. He cherishes his friends deeply, and no one can take that away from him. Good for you, Tiger!

But Tiger understands that he is a very public figure, a person of the world and for the world. He is recognized wherever he goes, and that reality can be a major plus; his image is only going to get bigger and bigger as his results on the PGA Tour continue to stand out. That's the inevitability of it all. Tiger's persona is going to just grow and grow. That's why it is so important for him to have some space to experientially develop while in his early 20s, because he is going to have much bigger and more complicated issues to deal with later in his life. He has got to develop that ability to handle adversity. I have faith that he will.

You see, Tiger carries with him a lot more social responsibility than the average 22-year-old eligible bachelor, because he represents a sport that has an ultraconservative image, a game with a very stringent code of ethics and conduct. Unlike other sports where young athletes are allowed to act their ages, express their individuality and sometimes get a little wild, golf offers no such latitude. Let's face it, the ruling bodies of golf are steeped in a very conservative history, and there hasn't been a very receptive attitude for the rock-star type of treatment that Tiger has received wherever he goes. I honestly believe they just aren't ready for a "happening" like Tiger.

His emergence into the professional golf world has begun to change golf's image from a stodgy, stuffy, country-club recreation, into a fun, exciting, diverse sport where everyone is free to be themselves. But that takes time. And until then, behavior that might be typical for a young man—so-called normal societal behavior—is not acceptable. It would be looked on with disfavor by the rulers of golf. I don't know how you tell a 21- or 22-year-old man to act like a saint, but that is exactly what certain factions of the media and the golf patriarchs want. And for whatever their reasons, they are *not* justifiable in my opinion.

How do you tell a 22-year-old man: "Don't go into a swimming pool and swim with beautiful women?"

How do you tell a 22-year-old not to go to nightclubs and dance?

You don't.

So Tiger stands alone from the other young athletes of his era, ethnicity aside, because more is expected of a young professional golfer than, say, a young pro basketball player or baseball player. In those sports, the press views young player conduct with a tongue in cheek permissiveness and shrug their shoulders: After all, boys will be boys, you know. But this kid Tiger is somehow held to a different standard, resulting in more intense scrutiny. Why? Because he represents the conservative game of golf. That's the only explanation or conclusion I can come up with—but I ask you, does that in itself then make it right?

When he attended Stanford University, Tiger publicly admitted his relationship with the media had been adversarial, but he was learning to handle the attention. The Stanford media head told me that there was more media interest in Tiger than in any previous Stanford athlete. Now that covers a lot of great players—Jim Plunkett, Tom Watson and John McEnroe to name just a few.

The media also began to learn he could not and would not grant every interview request.

"I'm trying to get adjusted to going to college and being away from home for the first time, and all the little nuances that come with going to college," Tiger explained in 1995. "And I kind of got a bad rap for that. After explaining it enough times, I think they finally understood."

Not only is Tiger besieged by the media, but reporters constantly are trying to pry personal information from his friends and relatives. We make it a practice not to divulge that type of information, so I have to wonder how some of our more personal data reaches public view.

Yet despite many attempts by the snoops to dig up some dirt on him, they haven't been able to come up with a thing. One of those gossip shows tried to create a romantic link between Tiger and Tyra Banks. Give me a break! My first reaction was: "Who the hell is Tyra Banks?" I had never even heard of her. Then I found out she was this fantastic-looking model, and I could sense that the media was again trying to create something where nothing existed.

For some strange reason there is open season on celebri-ties. They are like prey in a jungle, and anybody with a camera for a rifle can hunt them. They have long-range cameras, and they have short-range cameras. It is an open license to hunt, and hunt they do!

I only hope the paparazzi photographers will capture Tiger's positive actions as zealously as they do when they try to spot a misstep. Most of those photographers have no concern or appreciation for the rights of anyone else. Just for fun, I'd like someday to put the snoops under the identical surveillance they impose upon the stars they follow: have someone follow them home, take pictures of them and their families when they're not looking and create "special feature stories" based on anonymous "tips." Then blare their whole personal life out on the world and let them see what it feels like. But then, who would care?

Fortunately, Tiger hasn't been bothered by the photographers too much because of his clean image. He doesn't do a lot that's worth photographing, other than golf.

We can't address the paparazzi without mentioning the tragic death of Princess Diana, whose life epitomized what it was like to be hounded constantly by the media. Princess Diana related to the people of the world and through her actions and deeds clearly demonstrated that she cared for them. She admitted to having the same human frailties that common folks had. As a result, they could empathize totally with her shortcomings. The automobile accident that took her life was such a tragedy, such a waste. Here was someone intent on doing such good things for the world, and it was all snuffed out by this crazed thirst for "dirt." It's pitiful.

I have to wonder where it will all lead with Tiger. Will he be hounded and hounded until someone, somewhere, finds a shred of something questionable, just to discredit him? What's the prize? To be able to say, "See, he's not perfect"? Well, I'll save you the trouble and tell you right now, he's *not*! Neither am I, and furthermore neither are you! No one is! Those who insist on nit-picking at him persistently will have a long wait before he flinches. It's been tried, and it didn't work.

In an eight-page story in the April 1997 *Gentleman's Quarterly* magazine, a writer "revealed" what he apparently thought was big news: that en route to a one-hour photo shoot in a limousine, Tiger used profanity and told a few off-color jokes. Big deal!

The entire article revolved around this so-called incredible observation that Tiger was just a typical 21-year-old. I guess that was shocking to him. I don't know why he didn't just ask us—we would have been happy to tell him. Tiger professes to be nothing more, nothing less. But he also took some cheap shots at me, and that is where Tiger drew the line. He was furious after reading the article and reacted by releasing a statement through his agents at IMG:

"It's no secret that I'm 21 years old and that I'm naive about the motives of certain ambitious writers. The article proves that, and I don't see any reason for anyone to pay $3 to find that out. It's easy to laugh it off as juvenile and petty, except for the attacks on my father. I don't understand the cheap shots against him. For the writer to characterize my father as being 'cranky' about needing heart bypass surgery and ridicule him because fans like him is beyond my comprehension."

When it comes to the future scrutiny of Tiger, I hope the media will take a more sensible, less sensational but mature approach and conclude: "You know, we really have something special here. Let's not ruin it for the game, because the game is bigger than Tiger or anyone else in it. Let's preserve the integrity and popularity of the game. Let's start trying to be more objective by putting events in a little better perspective."

Athletes and celebrities are human beings. They are going to have arguments with their wives or girlfriends. They are going to make mistakes in judgment. That sort of thing happens to all people. But Tiger is going to be around in the public eye for the next 20 or 30 or 40 years, and the press needs to do its share to make it a lot easier on everybody. Hopefully the media can settle in and say, "You know, this kid is great for the game. We couldn't have asked for anything better."

I am still appalled by the excessive number of reporters who took "pot shots" at Tiger last year. It seemed to me like everything he did left him open to criticism and sarcasm. Tiger understands that life in the public eye means incredible scrutiny and often in-depth analysis of everything he does, but it's hard to understand how people can pick so hard on a young guy in his very first year as a professional and who is just getting started. In our society, we tend to build our athletes up ostensibly just so we can tear them down. This is stupid. One day he is the greatest hero in the world for winning the Masters by a record-shattering 12 strokes, and the next day he is target practice. There are golfers scattered through every tour in the world with problems far worse than Tiger's, believe me. Just consider his flaws along with his accomplishments and let's get on with life. There are more important things!

I truly hope something positive comes from the death of Princess Diana and the overly intense media scrutiny she and other celebrities have had to endure. Controls are urgently needed, because these overly aggressive media types have run amuck for too long. They need to be controlled, because they feel athletes and other public figures are open season. The attitude of "I can do anything I want" in the interest of, or under the guise of, freedom of the press is wrong. There are those that are abusing that privilege.

Don't get me wrong, I have a great deal of respect for the press—I was an information officer in the service and I have dealt with the press for years and years. I know the press has an internal code and that it wants to do the right thing. But just as society has its miscreants, there is a small element of the press that will do anything to get their name out in the limelight by breaking a story with information that no one else has, regardless of how harmful it might be to someone else. They figure it is fair game.

Well, I don't know which is worse: those factions of the press who drag everything into public view, or those factions of the golf community who keep some very dark secrets.

I keep reading stories that Augusta is tailor-made for Tiger, as if he only performed well there because of the course and not because of his skill. Well, Augusta is tailor-made for a lot of guys. Then, when Tiger had trouble later in the year, we even read that his game is not suited for major championship courses. Well, I have a news flash. The first year of his pro career was for adjustments and learning. Now let's watch him make his move in 1998 and see what he has learned. If it takes a couple more seasons, so what? Every level he has played on, he has done gone through the same scenario. It would not surprise me if Tiger made these adjustments and in 1998 won two or possibly three majors. Whatever happens, you can be sure the media will be there to capture every moment.

When I think back to the days of Arnold Palmer as a young player, or Jack Nicklaus as a young player, it shocks me to think how different things were for them. The media respected them, protected them, treated them as heroes. No one ever delved into their personal lives. Maybe it's the by-product of our changing times, where the media is far more pervasive than it was years ago. Maybe Tiger has been singled out because he is so unique. I don't know the answer.

But we do know the rules, and we understand that when you're a public figure, you're fairly powerless to strike back. So you close ranks, conduct yourself with dignity and surround yourself with people you truly trust. That is why his traveling entourage usually includes long-trusted friends from college and home. Tiger doesn't have any running buddies on Tour as yet, primarily because he is somewhat of an anomaly. He is the new kid on the block—a 22-year-old international superstar who also happens to be black and Asian. There simply aren't a lot of other guys on Tour who can automatically connect with Tiger on anything other than the love of the sport. Friendships on the tour will develop with time as Tiger and the other players get to know one another better. The Ryder Cup experience will contribute to that process.

For the most part, Tiger is fairly defensive in nature when it comes to meeting new people. And given his situation, that's probably a good thing; it precludes people from taking advantage of him. It is a constant battle. You have to watch your back.

When it comes to socializing, my advice to Tiger is: "Never, ever go out by yourself. Always have a friend with you. You need someone to watch your back, for one thing. And you must always have a witness, because somewhere there's a jerk who's going to try to set you up. He's going to get you alone, start something, and the next thing you know, he'll accuse you of hitting him. And he will have his friends backing him up, and you'll have no witness. So make sure you always have a buddy who can observe what's going on."

I have given thought to hiring a bodyguard to travel with Tiger, as many celebrities have found to be necessary. There's a pro and a con to it, because despite the protection, you really do sacrifice your personal freedom. So I decided against it last year, but will revisit that issue if it becomes necessary.

At one point last year, Tiger felt he needed to find a way to get to know some of the other players on the Tour, and let them get to know him. This is not easy because you're not talking about a large team where you live together, travel together and eat together. On tour, everyone goes his own way and you get to know your colleagues over the long haul. So Tiger went out of his way to be friendly and unpretentious, which should have been pretty natural for him, since he is both.

First, though, he had to maneuver through the PGA's unwritten, unspoken but understood caste system, which generally dictates that the Class A players, such as Tiger, usually don't play with the lesser ranked players in practice or tournament rounds and such. They don't associate with them. Well, what Tiger has done is make an effort to have fellow Class A players play with him in practice rounds, so they can get to know him better. His hope is that they will begin to pass the word down the line that Tiger is a good guy and an approachable person. You know, like a human being.

Apparently, it's working. I asked Tiger last fall how it was going and he said, "The guys are starting to know me a lot better, because the word is starting to filter down to them about what type of a person I am."

If there is any advantage to the huge amount of publicity he receives, it is that the media attention provides him a forum to espouse his beliefs and causes throughout the world. Tiger is concerned about improving the game, and he has reached out his hand to the former ambassadors of golf—Jack Nicklaus and Arnold Palmer—to get their wisdom and guidance about how he can carry the torch. Tiger and Arnold have shared a long, great relationship.

"More than a torch is being passed," Tiger said, "It's knowledge that's being passed on. I've had a chance to sit down with Arnie, and he's given me a lot of advice."

Tiger meets Jack Nicklaus for the first time at Bel Aire Country Club in Los Angeles, where Jack was conducting a clinic and Tiger put on a ball-striking exhibition. Only 15 at the time, Tiger was amazed that he was already taller than Jack. His feet didn't touch the ground for a month.

After playing with Tiger, Lehman and Love, Palmer graciously said: "I'm going to have an inferiority complex for three days after this."

The intensity of the public and media scrutiny of Tiger was unrivaled in 1997, and I would expect that high a degree of interest in him from the American public will continue. The same level of intensity will probably not hold, but I don't think people will lose interest in Tiger; the coverage he receives will likely continue to exceed the norm.

Many fellow golfers have alluded that Tiger maintains a sort of home-course advantage at virtually every place he plays because of the partisan gallery supporting him. But these large galleries present a double-edged sword. Tiger has to face the same distractions—the same amount of movement, the same amount of noise, the same crowd—as the others he's golfing with. So the only real advantage Tiger has is that he is accustomed to it. He can play in those conditions and put himself above those conditions, rather than have the conditions affect him. The disadvantage is that those crowds have unbelievably high expectations for Tiger, and he feels the pressure to play well in order to meet or exceed those expectations, or run the risk of that big crowd turning against him. The other disadvantage is that he is rarely the underdog. The other guy is usually the underdog. And people love to root for the underdog. As many fans as there are who love to see him win, there are fans who like to see him blow it once in awhile. So they can say, "See, even Tiger blows a shot."

Tiger's popularity on the course and his vast appeal to the masses already has effectively influenced the generally stiff protocol at golf tournaments: In future years, you'll start to see better security, tighter restrictions, and better conduct from the galleries as people who came to the course without prior knowledge of golf become more and more familiar with the game. It has become a learning experience for so many people who had never even been on a golf course before. These are not disruptive people; they just don't know when to cheer and not cheer. At the Western Open tournament in suburban Chicago last July, Tiger joked that there were fans who would cheer just because one of his shots got airborne, never mind whether it was a good shot or not.

Tiger is handling his celebrity just fine. He is doing real well, and I am proud of him. As his maturity increases he will be better able to handle the isolation he's going to face. Things can't and won't be like they were before he turned pro. He has got to figure out how to handle the lack of privacy, the invasion of privacy, and to understand that he can't just go wherever he wants and do whatever he wants. That's a tough thing for a kid. And let's not forget, he is still a kid.

Tiger understands that there are restrictions on his life that he has no control over, and he just has to accept them. His major strength continues to be his inherent knowledge of who he is.

His impact on the golf world is considerable. He had to come to an accommodation with his lifestyle, balance it, put it into perspective and then handle it all by himself, because there was nothing that I as a parent could do. That had to come from him.

After the Buick Classic in Atlanta in 1997, I made some suggestions for improvement, and Tiger said to me: "I have already made most of those adjustments, basically, and I accept all of the responsibility." Okay, I thought, that's great.

Then Tiger went home to Orlando.

The next week, he called me in California while I was having breakfast at the kitchen table. Tiger said: "You know, Pop, I had a soul-searching session last night. I looked at myself and said, 'Tiger, grow up.' I decided to act more professionally and mature. I feel as if I matured overnight. I really feel I have come to grips with not only the media situation, but also my role as a professional golfer and a celebrity. I have accepted the status, and I'm going to stop fighting it. I have grown a lot just overnight, Pop."

And then he added, "Thanks, Pop, for giving me the space to grow and to make my own mistakes. I knew you would be there all the time. But I had to go through it myself. I just want you to know how much I appreciate your allowing me to do that."

A parent can't ask for anything more than that.

Chapter Eleven

PLAYING THROUGH

As WE BEGAN planning for the 1998 Tour, we had to ask ourselves, what had we learned the previous year? What could we change? Where was room for improvement? And what we should leave alone sounds simple. Look here, snip there, add wherever.

There are certain things that will not change. Primarily, our goals and values are right where we need them to be, and you will not see those waver. Tiger will continue to make important contributions to society, and do everything in his power to advance the game of golf. I will continue to act as his lightning rod and take a lot of the heat for the decisions we make about his career. We will continue to make those decisions based on two criteria: First, everything we do must be in Tiger's best interest, and secondly, maintain the best image possible while always trying to do the right thing. That's important to me—that he does the right thing. It is not important that he win every tournament. If we accomplish keeping Tiger safe, happy and proud, that is fine with me. But if he ever loses sight of who he is and stops trying to be a good person and make contributions to others, then I will become very concerned and disappointed. If that was to happen, believe me, you would see Earl Woods step in and be a very vociferous father. You can believe that.

We learned a lot about Tiger's game under certain conditions, and what kind of adjustments we needed to make to improve his play. One area we continue to work on is his putting. It was evident to me that Tiger's putting problems toward the end of the season were caused in part by fatigue, which curtailed his desire to practice. But those struggles on the green were also a matter of technique.

Butch Harmon, Tiger's long-time swing coach, has been giving him putting advice. That has caused problems in the past. Tiger's putting style is so natural and simplistic that it's difficult for anyone to help him with it, other than the person who taught him—his dad. Over the years, he has repeatedly requested assistance from me to help on his putting, because I am the one who taught him how to putt in the first place. The style he utilizes is something you could teach a one-year-old who can't talk. It fits Tiger perfectly, because he is a "feel" putter. People call him a "power" player, but he is a "feel" putter.

Harmon, who worked with Tiger on his putting last year, is from the old so-called pop school of putting. But for whatever reason, that method doesn't seem to be working with Tiger, perhaps because Tiger was taught using a completely different method, by his own Pop. We resolved the situation in January '98 by acknowledging that he should have a single teacher for putting. That person is me. So far it has worked very well. He is right on track. Two timely lessons at the Mercedes produced a third-place finish. A single session assisted in his win at the Johnnie Walker Asian Classic over Ernie Els in January 1998. A well-timed lesson Friday evening at the Nissan Open this year resulted in a 65, 66 finish, tied for first place. As the season moves along we will be able to further stabilize his putting. This is what Tiger wanted—to go back to his old putting style. Told you the boy was not dumb; I've always ribbed him that he's a slow learner.

When Tiger was very young, reporters used to get ticked off at him when they asked him for details about his round of golf.

They would say, "On Number 4, how long was that putt?"

And Tiger would say, "I don't know."

And they'd say, "Ah, come on, Tiger, you know how long that putt was."

"No, I really don't," Tiger would answer.

You see, he doesn't putt for distance. He doesn't have a 20-foot pop, a 15-foot pop, a 10-foot pop. He putts to a "picture" and lets his natural athletic instincts take over. He just looks at the hole, and instead of coming back with a number in his head, he comes back with a picture of a distance that has no number on it. His mind automatically reads that distance. Then he applies a requisite force to get the ball there. It's a little more complicated than that, but I didn't say I was going to tell you everything.

I taught Tiger this method before he could barely talk. I said to myself: "How are you going to teach putting to a kid who doesn't know two inches from five miles?"

So I thought, "How about putting to a picture?"

I started off with him taking the ball in his right hand and rolling it to the hole. Then we proceeded further: "OK, now close your eyes and roll the ball to the hole."

Then I asked, "What did you see before you rolled the ball to the hole?"

He said, "I saw the hole."

"Now roll it to the hole again," I said. His distances were the same, no change.

At that point I said, "All you have to do is take your set-up stance, aim your putter, take a look at the hole and look at the ball. And look at the hole, which is the picture, and look at the ball. You will see that picture in your mind. Now roll the ball to the picture."

And that's the way he learned how to putt.

It's a very simplistic method, I know, but it's potential for success is based on natural athletic instinct, not technique. If you don't have the instinct, you'd better get some technique. But Tiger has incredible instincts.

He is an instinctive putter. I know it. It has become increasingly evident to me that when he veers away from his original style, he gets caught up in mechanics, and he misses.

Throughout last season, whenever Tiger sent up an SOS for help, it was more likely than not about his putting. We finally agreed that we would work together for awhile, so he could decide what was the best way for him to go. Now that I'm healthy again, I gave him the option of having me travel with him more, just to work with him on his practice rounds on the greens, so he can better get the feel and pace of the practice greens and so forth. When I used to accompany Tiger on trips during his amateur career, I taught him that you can't really prepare for putting until you get to the tournament greens. Working on those tournament site greens, his putting would get better and better every day. Last year, Tiger got away from that concept, and I feel it had something to do with the fact that I wasn't around. Too many different sources were telling him how to putt, and in the end, it messed him up.

When a golfer is not putting well, it affects the rest of his game. Especially with Tiger, you can tell by his reactions after his approach shots. You know he is saying to himself: "I'm not hitting the ball close enough to give myself a chance for a birdie."

Well, that puts pressure on your iron game. And if you are not in the short fairway grass, it puts pressure on your driving, too. If you are not getting the ball in the best position with your irons . . . it works its way all the way back to your driver.

Putting is a key element of the golf game where you can really shave strokes off your score. You may never again be able to substantially change the distance you can hit the ball, but you can always improve your putting stroke. Putting is a skill that seems to come and go—now you've got it, now you don't. It truly is an art form. But it's so crucial to your success. I don't care how close you hit the ball to the hole on your approach, you still have to putt it in.

Tiger's putting is going to mature as he gets more experience on the Tour and becomes more familiar with the greens at each stop. Don't forget, 90 percent of the courses Tiger played in 1997 were courses he played on for the very first time. He didn't know them at all, and there was no way to become familiar with them in advance.

The Masters was different. Not only had he played the course as an amateur, he had also watched a mountain of film of Augusta National, going back 10 years. He taped those particular holes that television covered and studied where and how the greens putted under all different conditions. Then when he went there, all he had to do was learn the holes that weren't covered on television in previous years. That's how he gave himself an advantage on that course in 1997. He had some cumulative experience on those greens. Makes a huge difference.

But I believe the critical point for Tiger at the Masters came the night before the tournament began, when he asked me: "What do you think of my putting stroke, Pop?"

I thought for a moment and said, "I don't like it."

That got his attention. "What do you mean?" he asked. "I'm having trouble seeing the line, but I played with Ben Crenshaw today, and Ben said that was the prettiest stroke he had seen out here in years."

I said, "Well, I don't like it. And here is what I would suggest that you do." I told Tiger three different things to do.

And he said, "Oh, I like that."

The next day, he went out there in the warm-up and tried my suggestions. And the rest is history. He had no three-putt greens in four days at Augusta. And he even publicly acknowledged that I had given him a putting lesson.

But I'm a firm believer that you should have instruction coming at you only from one direction.

Other changes? I look for Tiger to improve in 1998 with his new equipment. Last year, his iron clubs really took a beating, and by mid-season, they were pretty worn down. Yet like many golfers, he was reluctant to change clubs in the middle of the season, because you don't know how new clubs are going to feel. Now, for 1998, he has some beautiful new interchangeable iron clubs from Titlelist, and they really make a difference. He had a driver specially made for him over the winter, and I think those new clubs will really contribute to his overall performance.

As far as his tournament schedule, the PGA Tour and everybody else would like Tiger to play in more tournaments in '98, but you can only spread water so thin. Yes, it would be nice to play in more tournaments, but at what cost? In order to please everyone, you would have to play in every tournament, and that is not only unreasonable, it's just not good for Tiger. We do try to schedule him so that he can defend his titles, such as at the Western Open in suburban Chicago, as a courtesy to the tournament. But as I said earlier, we know now that he needs at least two consecutive weeks off between tournaments, and we're going to stick to that plan until we feel otherwise. I fully expect people to be upset about it, and I'm very happy to take the blame.

Or, if you like, you can call Tiger's agent, Hughes Norton, at IMG, who has also been an excellent buffer against people trying to persuade Tiger to play in more tournaments. We are in complete agreement about what is best for Tiger, and I'm grateful to have him on our team. The fact that he shares our priorities and strategies has made things go that much more smoothly for us all.

I'm sure it hasn't always been easy for Hughes, since he is part of an organization—IMG—that is extremely successful at creating more opportunities for its clients, not turning them down. Yet we have put Hughes and his colleagues in the position of turning down just about every opportunity that has been offered to Tiger, and believe me, there have been plenty. That has undoubtedly cost them millions of dollars in commissions. But Hughes and the others at IMG, so far, have been in complete agreement with our philosophy about how to manage Tiger's time and activities; they see the long-term picture. They understand that the top priority is what is in the best interest of Tiger, not the bottom line, not money. None of this is about money. It never has been and never will be—at least not for us.

The one thing Tiger has devoted endless and selfless time to is the Tiger Woods Foundation, which had its origin in 1997 trying to give kids of all ethnicities a chance to play golf the way Tiger did.

The Foundation was the mutual brainchild of Tiger and me, the result of personal conversations we had over the years, as Tiger participated in various tournaments. We would talk about what we were going to do in the future. It was part of his education; I felt it was essential that he learn early the importance of being socially responsible. To share and to care. Those are the two key words that we have in the Woods family—you share and you care.

I am the president of the Tiger Woods Foundation, but Tiger is the guiding light, driving force and spirit behind the organization. My assessment of the operation of the Tiger Woods Foundation is that the tail is wagging the dog. Tiger is the tail, and when he wags, everything happens. He goes at such a fast pace that it is hard for everybody to keep up with him.

When I think of what the Foundation has done in its first year, it is unbelievable. Other people in the foundation business look at us and say the same thing. We have learned from our mistakes and acknowledged that we were not immune from making mistakes. We moved on and got stronger and better as a result of our experiences. I am proud of what we did.

Now, long before we had an official name, a logo and a group of devoted people helping us with our Foundation, even before Tiger went to college, we used to put on clinics for kids.

That is where it all started. Unfortunately, the clinics were interrupted during his college years by the NCAA—they wouldn't let him do it. But we reinstituted the clinics when Tiger became a free man again and turned professional, as a way to give back to the kids and the communities.

Right away, we had a problem with the National Minority Golf Foundation, which is supposed to be the umbrella organization that provides flow-down support to local junior programs with funding from the USGA and the PGA Tour. Unfortunately, at the same time that the Tiger Woods Foundation was exploding onto the scene, they lost their leadership and had become somewhat ineffective. So there was a concern on the part of the National Minority Golf Foundation that we might start to receive the money they counted on to run their programs.

So I had a conversation with their legal counsel, who is a member of the executive board of the USGA, and I assured him that we had no intention of taking their funding, and that we would confine our participation in the golf arena to golf clinics. It would be our goal to act as a lightning rod to stir up and generate overall interest and participation in golf. We would not be a threat or a recipient of any funding efforts from the USGA or the PGA Tour. This understanding is in place today. Unfortunately, the organization has not evolved into what they want it to be. And they have not received their funding, so they cannot provide flow-down support to the local programs as was originally designed. So they are in a state of limbo right now, until monies start coming to them and they can do their job. Golf really needs them.

We were able to do our job because we got our funding support from Tiger and his corporate sponsors. We didn't have to initially depend on anyone else. We went out on a limb and incurred tremendous expense to put on six clinics in 1997, so Tiger could reach out to kids all over the country. And it worked.

We bit off a lot when we decided to put on those six clinics, since the organization was only about three months old. We had to hire people, and we went blindly into these communities—Chicago, Orlando, Dallas, Memphis, Miami and New York—not knowing exactly what we'd be facing. The clinics had to be organized on the local level as far as getting all of the support and participation from the various organizations in that city. It was a tremendous achievement to be able to pull it off. And I think we were very ambitious in doing six of them the first year. We are getting better every time we do it.

We have a format that we use. We go into a city and we say: "What we would like to do is to reward your selected children to receive hands-on instruction from Tiger." Then these local organizations select 25 or 30 kids who receive personalized instruction from Tiger. The balance of the children and their parents are then treated to an exhibition of ball-striking ability and a talk and question-and-answer period from Tiger. And, of course, I can't pass up an opportunity to get in a few words of my own. Tiger directs his talks to the kids; I speak to the parents. It is so important for children to hear adults talking about the job we have to do as parents, to know that their parents are there to help and care. To know that we are all trying to improve the relationship between the parents and their children.

The message delivered by Tiger to these kids is that nobody owes you anything, and that you can learn an awful lot about life and yourself through the game of golf. Tiger tells the children: "Look, there are no shortcuts in golf, and there are no shortcuts in life. You have to work for it. Dream big and keep your dreams for yourself. Because the dreams that you have are those things that separate you from others. If you give up your dream, you give up hope. And without hope, you are nothing."

Tiger always has been taught that when you share and you care for others, you invariably help yourself, because it makes you a better person. *To give is not a choice—it is an obligation.* And when you come from this deep sense of personal self-worth that Tiger does, then you have the capacity to give. And the beautiful part of it all is that the children in the clinics know it. They recognize it. They know Tiger is for real. Tiger gives them a role model for doing what is good and what is right in their community and improving themselves and their lot, instead of giving up hope and succumbing to drugs and crime and all the other associated problems that exist in the inner-city.

I call Tiger the Pied Piper. You see, children know when people are honest and sincere and truthful. And they listen. He says to the kids: "I am going to open my heart to you today." And you can hear the silence grow. The kids are just waiting with bated breath. Nobody says anything. All movement ceases. Attention is riveted on Tiger. And he challenges them to be a role model for others. He says: "I was selected as a role model. I didn't volunteer for this, but I accepted it and I am doing the best I can with the abilities that I have. You can, too. You can be a role model to someone else. Adopt someone else. Share yourself. Give to others and grow from the experience."

Tiger challenges them to push their own limits and make positive contributions. And they sit there in rapt attention and get the message.

When I talk to the parents, I say: "Look, Tiger challenged your children to do this. At the very least, I am challenging you to be a role model for your children. And to share and care with others. Make yourself a better person. Make other people better people. If your children can do it, you can do it, too."

And the beautiful thing is this: As I make those comments and look at the faces in the crowd, I see parents nodding yes, yes, yes. And most times I get standing ovations and am interrupted by applause. (Tiger always gets standing ovations!) You are hitting a nerve and you are hitting it hard. And the message is being received. It is the start of making a difference.

I tell the parents this: "What I try to do each and every day of my life is to make a difference in one person's life. If we can do that on an individual basis, think what a different world this would be. What we, the foundation, want to do is improve the relationship between one parent and one child. If we can do that, if we can make the lot of the child better, then we have made a difference in that child's life. And in that parent's life, too."

If somehow we can affect a whole bunch of these relationships, then we have improved a whole neighborhood. If you improve a bunch of neighborhoods, you improve a city. You improve a group of cities and you improve a nation. And when you improve a group of nations, you improve the world. You have made a difference. It all starts with a single relationship between one parent and one child. We are driven to succeed.

As we begin our second year of operation, we plan to con-

Tiger hosts a golf clinic for inner-city kids at the Phoenix Open. Note my granddaughter Cheyenne is all eyes front-and-center as she takes in the instruction. The event was not one of the official Tiger Woods Foundation clinics for 1997. It was hosted by the Thunderbirds of Phoenix.

Tiger studies the swings of future competitors.

Lessons of caring and sharing are passed on by Tiger at his Tiger Woods Foundation golf clinic. Children and parents listen attentively.

I'm a Tiger, he's a Tiger—we're all Tiger's kids.

tinue the clinics on a selective basis. Last year's events were planned to coincide with a PGA Tour tournament, so Tiger didn't have to travel in excess, and so we could facilitate his participation. The two final clinics were added where Tiger had no tournament, but we figured it would be late enough in the season that Tiger would be well on the way by then to adjusting to the PGA Tour in his first year. Now, in the foundation's second year, we are soliciting and encouraging bid proposals from many cities who are seeking a Tiger Woods clinic for their communities. Hopefully, Tiger will be better adjusted to the Tour in his second year and we can devise a schedule that permits him to do clinics on a Sunday when he doesn't have a tournament, or on a Monday following a tournament.

No question, the 1998 PGA season will be an important year for the game of golf. One of the things that has been a recurring problem in my mind is: What are we going to do with these new golf enthusiasts who flock to the courses to play golf or to watch other golfers?

Each Tiger Woods Foundation golf clinic features a ball-striking exhibition by Tiger. This clinic was at Disney World and was the first of six conducted in 1997.

Under the watchful eye of Tiger, clinic participants practice and receive personal instruction.

Clinics always feature autograph sessions as Tiger obliges his young fans.

After a busy morning on the links, the young participants enjoy a well-deserved break for lunch.

In a speech at a Phoenix clinic last year, I challenged the rulers of golf to come up with a plan for a place for these kids to practice and play at an affordable rate. And last November, I participated in major public announcements in New York, Detroit and Houston about the development of a plan and a partnership between the PGA Tour, the Tiger Woods Foundation and the major golf organizations in the United States, to build 200 golf learning centers in the *inner-cities* by the year 2000. It is called the First Tee Initiative. This is going to be one of the biggest things in golf in the last 50 years. Whoever heard about the game of golf concerning itself with the inner-city? It is a complete change of philosophy, and it is a credit to Tim Finchem, the PGA commissioner, and his leadership and his foresight. It's going to be thrilling to watch it all unfold, as countless people in the cities have new opportunities to play a sport that's never before been available to them.

Our intention at the Foundation is to eventually devote less time to promoting golf, and more to our principal area of concern, the sociological and the humanitarian issues facing our society with special emphasis on parenting. Right now, our efforts are concentrated in the United States, but as we grow and develop and expand and have access to more money, we plan to expand our activities worldwide, again addressing sociological and humanitarian issues. Our first effort will probably be directed toward the Pacific Rim region, due to Tiger's Asian cultural heritage. Someday, it is conceivable that we could make a contribution to an educational system in Bangladesh, for example, or anything we dream of doing. These are our general plans. We recognize that golf is a worldwide sport now. And through Tiger's popularity and his success in golf, there are going to be innumerable opportunities for him to make a contribution and a difference in places that no one would even imagine before.

Yes, it is far-reaching. It is pretty big in scope. But I have a firm belief that if you don't dream big, you don't achieve big. And that is our dream—to make a big difference. We have received tremendous encouragement. All of Tiger's endorsers, as a matter of choice, have voluntarily supported the foundation in financial terms, and with equipment and golfing items. And they are in full support of our goals and objectives. And as we expand beyond the arena of golf, we will also expand our support base into worldwide manufacturers and worldwide corporations who want to make a difference and want to assist and help.

Tiger is the spokesperson and catalyst; golf is the platform and a medium for social change and assistance. There is no doubt in my mind that the sport of golf creates the perfect forum for an individual athlete to take a stand and decide for himself what he wants to do in the world. In team sports—basketball, football, baseball—even the top athletes (and certainly the average ones) have certain unspoken restrictions on what they can say or do, simply because someone else pays their salaries. Someone else controls their destiny, whether it's the coach or the owner or even his own teammates. Coaches' decisions can set you on the bench and you don't play. If your ideas about social reform don't coincide with the owner's, you can be traded and saddled with the stigma of being a troublemaker.

But in golf, every player is an individual entrepreneur. You work for yourself. No coach can sit you down and demand that you keep your mouth shut "for the good of the team." No owner can threaten to not renew your contract. So you have the unprecedented freedom to speak out—to make a difference.

I would love to see other athletes take a more active stance on social issues; every voice increases the likelihood that something good will happen. And I would encourage them to do that. Because goodness knows we have enough social problems to go around for everybody to address.

If all of this sounds a bit ambitious for a 22-year-old who happens to play golf for a living, don't worry. Tiger is a dreamer, but he is also very thorough, very prepared. He plans way in advance, and the foundation is indicative of how he does it. Golf does not have to worry about Tiger leading it astray. He has too much respect for the game of golf, and for the people who have contributed so much to its development and popularization. He is just going to take it to another level that it has never known before.

And for those who see Tiger as some sort of a threat to the game of golf—and there are plenty who feel that the attention he receives is extreme and somehow detrimental to the sport— I say look at him as a positive instrument for change. His stature and his status allow him to improve the game for all golfers. Already the improved security, which we alone campaigned for, has benefited everyone on the tour. The entire game of golf is going to become financially richer, because of its increased popularity and visibility, due in large part to Tiger. He's not asking for a lot in exchange. All he wants is the chance to play the sport he loves, as well as he can possibly play it, and the chance to do some good things in the world. Would anyone begrudge him this? I hope not.

Tiger and the game of golf will continue to flourish in 1998, as the multitude of new fans learn more and more about the complexities of the game, the rules and idiosyncrasies, the customs and traditions. I think we'll see improved conduct in the galleries, and a continuing increase in the participation of people, especially minorities.

When it comes to accommodating the anticipated increase in fans at PGA venues in the future, tournament officials are going to have to institute better crowd control measures, because a golf course can only hold so many people. Last year, unprecedented numbers turned out at tournament sites, and they all seemed to be following the same guy. It got to the point that it was just physically impossible to see anything of Tiger at all. Now many fans are finding out what I knew all along: That in order to see Tiger play, you have to leap-frog and skip a hole where he is playing, so you can see him on the next hole. Rarely can you watch him on an entire hole, because you can't walk along with him. The crowds are just too dense. What a nice problem for golf to have.

But I have been pleased by increased security at the PGA Tour sites. And we're doing our part as well. For example, to satisfy the huge number of autograph seekers who turn out, we will schedule autograph sessions for Tiger at each tour site, maybe twice a week. Each tournament will have the responsibility of making sure that the line is cut off at the appropriate time, because Tiger's autograph lines will never end. So if he is scheduled to sign for 30 minutes, there will be a 30-minute line. We're doing this for the fans as well as for Tiger; there's nothing worse than looking into the faces of people who have stood in line for hours for an autograph, only to be told Tiger isn't signing any more that day. It's a bad experience for everyone and definitely a lose-lose situation.

Tiger has been accustomed to signing autographs since he

was about 15 years old, especially for kids. Of course, since last year, he's had some real mob scenes to deal with, but he has really learned how to handle it. Part of that process was Tiger maturing; it has made it easier for him to cope. In the future, the maturation process will continue, and hopefully security measures will get even better. Michael Jordan tells Tiger that there is no solution to the extensive attention he will get from fans. Michael tells Tiger: "What works for you is what you have to insist on."

One place Tiger has always been mobbed is at airports, and so now we buy time on a private fleet of jets. It is a business expense that is absolutely necessary for his peace of mind: He can come and go when he pleases, without worrying about missing a flight or scheduling another. And there is no way that he can go into a commercial airport terminal anymore, without creating problems for himself and for everybody else, especially security, so the best thing for him has been private aircraft, and he flies that way exclusively. When he arrives at a site, the limo can drive right out to the runway and pick up the bags. It even works internationally, because they have people from the customs division to meet passengers of the private planes.

Everyone needs and deserves some privacy, no matter who they are. And this year, I hope Tiger can find a little privacy in his life. People always ask his mother and me about whether he has a girlfriend, if he's seeing anyone. Well, if I had an answer to that, I wouldn't write about it in my book—I'll leave that up to him. But I will say this: When Tiger chooses to take a mate for life, he will have the benefit of hearing about my experiences in that department, and we have had many long, important conversations on the subject. I have told him about my failed first marriage, and I have shared with him the pain, the anguish, the frustration that I had in that relationship. I have also talked with him about my marriage to his mother, and the realities of that relationship, good and bad. I have shared with him my experiences, what to look for, how to look for certain qualities. He is so much better prepared than I was at age 22 to select a mate.

But as far as Tiger is concerned, there are two areas of his life I am not going to get involved in: One is his selection of a caddie, because choosing a caddie is like choosing a soulmate, and you have to do that yourself, as Tiger did when he chose Michael "Fluff" Cowan. The other area I will not be involved in is his choice of a mate.

Of course, we talk about the kind of a person he is going to need to support him. I believe that behind every successful superstar, you will find a spouse who is supportive. But choosing the actual woman is up to him, as it should be.

Now, from his mother's perspective, Tida is very protective of Tiger. Obviously, she wants him to have the best. And I don't know if there is ever going to be a woman good enough for him in her eyes. But he will have to deal with that.

Tida innocently kicked off a minor controversy in Thailand in 1997, when local reporters at a news conference questioned her about whether Tiger might someday marry a Thai woman, and she was incorrectly quoted as saying she would prefer if he did.

Tiger didn't even have a girlfriend, but the subject kicked up a dust storm of interest, and when Tiger arrived at the Asian Honda Classic, he was forced to address the issue with a crowded press conference.

"I will marry who I fall in love with," Tiger said, hoping to dismiss the topic.

When he arrived at the Bangkok airport, his mother told him, "Welcome home."

He couldn't wait to find out what she had really said. "Mom, did you say that? It's all over the world."

"No," Tida told Tiger. "I didn't say that. I had a press conference, and they asked, 'Is Tiger going to have a Thai wife?' I said it's up to him. He's the one that has to marry, not me. I'm not going to marry for him. You can't force it as a parent.

"The next day it's all over the world that I want Tiger to marry a Thai girl. Next time I'm going to tape record it. One press conference, and now look what happens." See, even mothers get picked on by the media.

When Tiger returned to Thailand in January of 1998, he was asked if he believed in romance and whether he hoped to settle down.

Tiger said: "I believe in it but just not right now. I'm kind of busy right now."

And is he ever. The first Tiger Woods Invitational tournament was held last November in Japan, and it was such a success we plan to make it an annual event. Japan had been trying to get Tiger to come over there since he was 8 years old, but I had never allowed it, because it would have interfered with his school year.

The Tiger Woods Invitational was three days of mini-tournaments held in western Tokyo, involving professional, amateur and junior golfers. Veteran PGA golfers Nick Price and Mark O'Meara, as well as Japanese golf star Shigeki Maruyama, took part in a one-day professional event, sponsored by Japanese and American firms. It was Tiger's first visit to Japan other than brief stopovers at airports. Tiger told the Japanese media he would pass on eating sushi, the Japanese delicacy featuring uncooked fish.

"I'm not a big fish eater. I'll take a Japanese cheeseburger if you have them," he said.

From there, he began planning his strategies for the upcoming Tour season. I've been asked countless times about how Tiger was going to approach the defending of his Masters title this year. It seems ironic to me, since a year ago people were saying that Tiger could never win at Augusta in only his first year on the tour. I'll never forget reporters asking: "How in the hell can Tiger win the Masters when he hasn't even broken par at Augusta yet? And after he missed the cut the previous year as an amateur. How can Tiger talk about winning the tournament?"

Well, first, he expects to win every tournament he enters. Even though he didn't play very well there the year before, Tiger expected to win his first Masters. Second, he's not worried about breaking his own record, or "topping" what he did last year. He's interested in playing well, and winning if he plays well enough. And third, he is one year closer to physical maturity; he still isn't there yet. I believe that when he's about 24, he will mature like Johnny Miller did. Miller was a string bean as a young man, and all of a sudden he weighed about 190 pounds. He matured late. Tiger is going to be the same way. Right now he tips the scales at 167 pounds with 5 percent body fat.

Among Tiger's goals for 1998, I think, is another PGA Player of the Year honor. As the youngest player ever to win the award, it was particularly significant for him in 1997, because it was his first full year, and it is voted on by the players. He also collected the Arnold Palmer Trophy as leading money winner, and that wouldn't be bad to repeat either.

And as the Chinese New Year rang in the Year of the Tiger in February, my Tiger's dramatic 1998 season-opening victory could be a good omen.

"It's really just another year. It just happens to have my name on it," Tiger said demurely after defeating South African Ernie Els on a dramatic last day of the Johnnie Walker Classic in Thailand. Tiger had forced a regulation tie, then beat Els on the second hole of a playoff with an indescribable 15-foot birdie putt.

Tiger's seven-under-par 65 was only one short of the course record, as Els, leader for three days, faltered at the end to drop into a playoff as both finished on 279, nine under par.

Defending champion Els, who closed with a 73 after shooting 74 in the third round, had to sink a 15-foot birdie putt on the last hole in the final round just to get into a shoot-out before Tiger's birdie at the second playoff hole earned him the $222,000 first prize.

"When Ernie bogeyed the 17th and hit his second on the 18th I decided not to even practice because I'd had [that same] putt earlier and didn't think there was any way he'd make it," said Tiger.

"I was in the clubhouse, but when [the putt] went in I immediately bolted for the practice tee. Then when I got there they didn't have any practice balls right away. I only had the chance to hit a few sand irons and eight irons and five drivers.

"I made sure I hit the last three as hard as I could to get the nervous energy out of me, but I was pretty pumped up at the first playoff hole. I hit a real big drive, then my approach shot went over the green.

"I then kind of hung in there by sinking the par putt. It was mighty important." No kidding. It was Tiger's eighth professional victory in only 17 months, including his four U.S. wins.

After his thrilling win in Thailand, Tiger began looking ahead to the four majors again.

"It's nice to win, but I want my game to be peaking for all the majors," he said. "When you look at all the great players, that's what they all focused on. It's hard to keep your game for all four, but they did it, and I want to also.

"The whole idea is to keep getting better each year, and I'd love to win every time I go out. But if I improve every year, it will be a great career, and that's what I'm striving for.

"Last year I had some faults and put them right, and this week has finally paid dividends for doing that."

But of course, even as Tiger was winning that first tournament of the 1998 PGA season with the remarkable comeback against Els, he was already facing skeptics.

Veteran South African Gary Player forecast that Els, his 28-year-old compatriot, would prove to have a more successful career than Tiger.

"In my opinion Ernie will be better in the long run than Tiger as long as he has the desire," Player said. "Ernie's short-game is better than Tiger's, that's why I think this. Hitting the ball prolific distances is not the be-all and end-all of golf. Seventy percent of success in golf comes from a hundred yards in, and Ernie has more finesse with his wedges and short game than Tiger.

"Both are so talented though, and I have great admiration for Tiger, and you have to also take into consideration that I am biased towards Ernie as a fellow-countryman. They are so good for the game. They stimulate it so much," Player added.

Interestingly, Els seemed less sure. The U.S. Open champion in 1997, Els made note of Tiger's statement that he needed to be more consistent despite winning the Masters and three other U.S. PGA Tour events to exceed $2 million in prize money.

"I wish I could be that inconsistent. Tiger thinks he can win every time he starts, and that's no bad thing," said Els.

It's all about confidence, and I pray that he never loses that. Tiger is an extremely powerful person, and he is just getting in touch with his own power. Believe me, we have not yet seen the full extent of his influence. But we will. He has the capacity to do infinitely more than I was ever able to do, by virtue of his platform and his timing, and his place in the world. I will be right there behind him, supporting him in his endeavors. We will play through together.

We even got the chance to play a little golf together recently, when Tiger and I were paired together at the AT&T National Pro-Am at Pebble Beach in late January 1998. The weather was atrocious, and the tournament was rained out, which turned out to be a blessing since I was getting tired of slogging through the mud and wet grass. But it was a real goal for us to be there together; last year he played with Kevin Costner instead because of my heart problems. He challenged me to be well enough to play with him this year, and I came through for us. What an absolute joy for both of us.

Since Tiger turned professional, I have noticed that the switch went back on in my competitive instincts; they seemed to have kicked back in. Now that I have the time and the opportunity, I like the idea of competing again. I have set a goal for myself, to get my handicap back down to where it once was—one. Right now, I feel that I'm not far away from being able to shoot par. It is just a matter of correcting a few things and becoming consistent. John Anselmo, one of Tiger's early teachers, told me recently that my swing is better than it was five years ago. So I have improved. But at the same time I have to acknowledge the aging process. Boy, don't we all. I don't hit it as far as I did before. But I can still putt and chip with Tiger. I compete with him on an equitable basis in those areas all of the time. And I'm pretty sure he's not letting me look good on purpose.

Tiger and I don't talk that often on the phone anymore, unless he really needs something. Our relationship is so solid and so secure that it doesn't need validating every day. We don't feel the need to communicate, because we know we are there for each other always. Even at tournaments, I can be at the site and talk to him only two or three times. That's it for the whole week, and we are usually staying in the same suite. He generally is in one room of the suite, with a living room separating us, and there I am in the other room. Yet, it is comforting enough for him to know that I am there. Regardless of his status, he still needs his space, and I give it to him.

I am an independent individual, yet I take very seriously my responsibilities to Tiger. And if I don't, who will? Who could Tiger count on? Nobody. He knows that I am protecting his back. He knows I am there 24 hours a day, covering for him.

I marvel at the idea of Tiger passing onto the entire world the very important lessons, perspectives and philosophies my mother taught to me in our small house in Manhattan, Kansas; it's like watching history flow before my eyes. The unlikely events of my own life somehow led me to be hitting golf balls into a net while my baby boy sat and watched. He somehow took advantage of that opportunity to learn the golf swing and become addicted to the game of golf. He doesn't just love the game, he's addicted to it. And through that love and addiction, he has the potential to become perhaps one of the greatest players ever to grace the game. And from that platform, he can share his beliefs and intrinsic values with fans and followers around the world, the same values I passed to him, that were passed to me by my mother. And it goes on. Golf is the vehicle, but golf is not the end result. That is not the end objective. The objective is helping people, improving the lives of people, giving back love, the motto of the Tiger Woods Foundation. He will utilize the game of golf to accomplish that.

We are not just talking about helping people in the cities of Chicago or New York or Birmingham. People are the same all over the world. There are problems galore. Each and every one of us deserves better. There *is* enough for all of us. And that's why it is so beautiful that this international game of golf is going to be the vehicle for Tiger to spread this word. It is the perfect sport. And it is growing in popularity and influence each day.

I can't help but wonder what Tiger's place in sports history will be 40 years from now.

Believe me, there is someone who knows, and He is orchestrating this whole thing. Somewhere behind the scenes, there is a plan at work here. I came to that conclusion a long time ago, as I watched mysterious circumstances unfold, inexplicable things that have defined both my life and Tiger's since he was a baby. I remember watching things happen, and thinking, "Wow! I didn't do that." And then Tiger would grow a little more, and something else would happen that I had no control over. And events just lined up like "7"s on a slot machine—bing, bing, bing, and then Jackpot! And Tiger just keeps gliding on through.

I finally stopped thinking of those occurrences as coincidence. I had to look back at my own life, and wonder why I had done certain things. Why had I chosen to go to Information Officers School in the Army? Now I know: to offer solid public relations counsel to Tiger. Why in the hell at the age of 35 would a guy like me go into the Green Berets? At the time I thought it was to get a fair shake. Wrong. Now I know why. It was meant to give me the tools to pass on mental toughness to Tiger. When Tiger was a boy, why was I fixated on getting Tiger a sports psychologist at a very young age? And why was it that in my own golf group, the guy I had been playing golf with almost every weekend for four years turns out to be a sports psychologist, Jay Brunza? And one who shared my dream for Tiger? Even he said to me, "Earl, this was not by accident. I was led to this point. I was led to interface with you and Tiger at this point in his life. I was prepared."

Tiger possesses infinitely more power than I have. He has the essence of good and sharing and caring. He has the ability to do so much more. To touch more people.

I would love to know where he is headed, and I hope I am here long enough to find out. I have no intention of leaving before I do. All I know is that He didn't waste all of this time preparing this little guy without some big purpose. And whatever it is, it is going to be profound. It is going to be powerful, and it is going to be magnificent. I encourage all of you to carefully watch it unfold.

A LETTER TO MY SON

THIS BOOK WOULD not be complete without the following "open" letter to my son Tiger. I herewith share it with you all.

Dear Tiger,

You are my little man. You are my treasure. God gave you to me to nurture and to grow and to develop. I always have had your interests first and foremost in my life, and it always will be. In fact you mean more to me than life itself. I can remember when I taught you that it was OK to cry—that men can cry. It was not a sign of weakness, but a sign of strength. That was part of the education and the legacy that I wanted to leave with you, that sharing and caring for others is a way of life. And it is not to be taken lightly. I pass on all of my abilities to share and to care to you. I realize that you have an infinite, higher capacity and capability to perpetuate this philosophy in our day's world. I trust that I have given you the guidance and love in which you can then execute that mission. What God has in mind for you, I don't know. It is not my call. It was my job to prepare you. I trust that I have done the best job that I can. I know you will give it your all. And that you will be my little man forever.

Love,

Pop *Pop*

TIGER WOODS' CAREER STATISTICS

1997 PGA Statistics

Tiger Woods faced high expectations during his first full year on the PGA Tour, winning four events, including the Masters. He struggled in the other three majors and the Ryder Cup. Other wins in 1997 came at the Mercedes Championship, Byron Nelson Classic and the Western Open. He was paired with Colin Montgomerie in the third round of the Masters and shot a 65 en route to a record 12 stroke victory.

- **1997 PGA Tour Events Played:** 21
- **Best Finish:** First place (Mercedes Championships, The Masters, Byron Nelson Classic, Western Open)
- **Cuts Made:** 20
- **Top 10 Finishes:** 9
- **Rounds Played:** 81
- **Rounds Under Par:** 47
- **Rounds in the 60s:** 34
- **PGA Tour Earnings:** $2,066,833

- **Career PGA Tour Earnings:** $2,857,427
- **Earnings Worldwide:** $2,440,832
- **Career Worldwide Earnings:** $3,373,076

PGA Player of the Year

In 1997, Tiger Woods added his name to the list of PGA Player of the Year Award winners after clinching the honor with two tournaments still to play. Following is a list of all-time winners of the PGA Player of the Year Award.

1948 Ben Hogan	1970 Billy Casper
1949 Sam Snead	1971 Lee Trevino
1950 Ben Hogan	1972 Jack Nicklaus
1951 Ben Hogan	1973 Jack Nicklaus
1952 Julius Boros	1974 Johnny Miller
1953 Ben Hogan	1975 Jack Nicklaus
1954 Ed Furgol	1976 Jack Nicklaus
1955 Doug Ford	1977 Tom Watson
1956 Jack Burke, Jr.	1978 Tom Watson
1957 Dick Mayer	1979 Tom Watson
1958 Dow Finsterwald	1980 Tom Watson
1959 Art Wall	1981 Bill Rodgers
1960 Arnold Palmer	1982 Tom Watson
1961 Jerry Barber	1983 Hal Sutton
1962 Arnold Palmer	1984 Tom Watson
1963 Julius Boros	1985 Lanny Wadkins
1964 Ken Venturi	1986 Bob Tway
1965 Dave Marr	1987 Paul Azinger
1966 Billy Casper	1988 Curtis Strange
1967 Jack Nicklaus	1989 Tom Kite
1968 No Award	1990 Nick Faldo
1969 Orville Moody	1991 Corey Pavin

1992 Fred Couples   1995 Greg Norman
1993 Nick Price   1996 Tom Lehman
1994 Nick Price   *1997 Tiger Woods*

1997 Top Money Winner

Tiger Woods, as a 21-year-old Tour rookie, set lofty standards for himself with a record-breaking performance in 1997, winning four tournaments and becoming the first PGA golfer to earn over $2 million in a single season. Woods earned the Arnold Palmer Trophy as the top money winner. Following are the leading money winners on the U.S. PGA Tour in 1997 (U.S. players unless stated):

1. *Tiger Woods—$2,066,833*
2. David Duval—1,885,308
3. Davis Love—1,635,953
4. Jim Furyk—1,619,480
5. Justin Leonard—1,587,531
6. Scott Hoch—1,393,788
7. Greg Norman (Australia)—1,345,856
8. Steve Elkington (Australia)—1,320,411
9. Ernie Els (South Africa)—1,243,008
10. Brad Faxon—1,233,505
11. Phil Mickelson—1,225,390
12. Jesper Parnevik (Sweden)—1,217,587
13. Mark O'Meara—1,124,560
14. Mark Calcavecchia—1,117,365
15. Loren Roberts—1,089,140
16. Vijay Singh (Fiji)—1,059,236
17. Nick Price (Zimbabwe)—1,053,845
18. Stuart Appleby (Australia)—1,003,356
19. Tom Lehman—60,584
20. Steve Jones—59,108

Tournament Performances By Year

Professional Career Record

1998

Tournament	Par	Round Scores	Total	Winnings	Finish
Mercedes Championships	72	72–67–69–64—272	16-under	$149,600	Tied 2nd
Buick Invitational	72	71–66–68—205	11-under	$109,200	Tied 3rd
Johnnie Walker Classic (European PGA)	72	72-71–71–65—279	9-under	$218,661	1st

1997

Tournament	Par	Round Scores	Total	Winnings	Finish
Mercedes Championships	72	70–67–65—202	14-under	$216,000	1st
Phoenix Open	71	68–68–67–72—275	9-under	$20,250	Tied 18th
Pebble Beach National Pro Am	72	70–72–63–64—269	19-under	$167,200	Tied 2nd
Asian Honda Classic	—	70–64–66–68—268	—	$48,450	1st
Australian Open	—	68–70–72–73—283	—	$15,548	Tied 8th
Nissan Open	71	70–70–72–69—281	3-under	$14,600	Tied 20th
Bay Hill Invitational	72	68–71–71–68—278	10-under	$42,000	Tied 9th

1997 cont.

Tournament	Par	Round Scores	Total	Winnings	Finish
Players Championship	72	71–73–72–73—289	1-over	$20,300	Tied 31st
The Masters	72	70–66–65–69—270	18-under	$486,000	1st
Byron Nelson Classic	70	64–64–67–68—263	17-under	$324,000	1st
The Colonial	70	67–65–64–72—268	12-under	$70,400	Tied 4th
The Memorial	72	72–75–74—221	5-over	$3,800	Tied 67th
U.S. Open	70	74–67–73–72—286	6-over	$31,915	Tied 19th
Buick Classic	71	72–72–71–72—287	3-over	$4,568	Tied 43rd
Western Open	72	67–72–68–68—275	13-under	$360,000	1st
British Open	71	72–74–64–74—284	even	$17,362	Tied 24th
Buick Open	72	72–68–70–68—278	10-under	$43,500	Tied 8th
PGA Championship	70	70–70–71–75—286	6-over	$13,625	Tied 31st
World Series of Golf	70	67–72–69–70—278	2-under	$114,400	Tied 3rd
Canadian Open	70	70–76—146	6-over	0	cut
Walt Disney Classic	72 72	66–71–70–71—278	10-under	$10,650	Tied 25th
Las Vegas Invitational	72	68–64–77–71–75—355	5-under	$8,663	Tied 33rd

1997 cont.

Tournament	Par	Round Scores	Total	Winnings	Finish
TOUR Championship	71	69–68–75–69—281	3-under	$97,600	Tied 12th
MasterCard PGA Grand Slam	72	66–70—136	8-under	$250,000	2nd
Skins Game	—	2 Skins	—	$40,000	3rd

Tiger Woods' professional career began in August 1996 at the Greater Milwaukee Open. His total winnings in 1996 placed him in the top 30 money winners for the entire year, which authorized him to play in the Tour Players Championship at year end. He won twice, at the Los Angeles Invitational and at Disney World, and he topped the year off with being voted by his peers PGA Rookie of the Year.

1996

Tournament	Round Scores	Finish
Greater Milwaukee Open	67–69–73–68—277	Tied 60th
Bell Canadian Open	70–70–68—208	Tied 11th
Quad City Classic	69–64–67–72—272	Tied 5th
B.C. Open	68–66–66—200	Tied 3rd
Las Vegas Invitational	70–63–68–67–64—332	1st
LaCantera Texas Open	69–68–73–67—277	3rd
Walt Disney/Oldsmobile	69–63–69–66—267	1st
Tour Championship	70–78–72–68—288	Tied 21st
Holden Australian Open	79–72–71–71—292	Tied 5th
Skins Game	—	2 Skins
J.C. Penney Classic	mixed team event	Tied 2nd

Amateur Career Record in Professional Events

1996

Tournament	Round Scores	Finish
The Masters	75–75—150	Missed Cut
U.S. Open Championship	76–69–77–72—294	Tied 82nd
Scottish Open	81–75—156	Missed Cut
British Open Championship	75–66–70–70—281	Tied 22nd

1995

The Masters	72–72–77–72—293	Tied 41st
U.S. Open Championship	74 (withdrew)	WD (Injury)
Motorola Western Open	74–71–79–69—293	Tied 57th
Scottish Open	69–71–75–78—293	Tied 29th
British Open Championship	74–71–72–78—295	Tied 68th

1994

Johnnie Walker Asian Classic	74–71–74–73—292	Tied 34th
Nestle Invitational	80–77—157	Missed Cut
Buick Classic	75–70—145	Missed Cut
Motorola Western Open	74–75—149	Missed Cut

1993

Tournament	Round Scores	Finish
Nissan Los Angeles Open	74–78—152	Missed Cut
Asian Honda Classic	72–78—150	Missed Cut
GTE Byron Nelson Classic	77–72—149	Missed Cut

1992

Tournament	Round Scores	Finish
Nissan Los Angeles Open	72–75—147	Missed Cut

INDEX

Tiger Woods Foundation, Inc.
OUR MISSION

The Tiger Woods Foundation envisions a world where people of varying backgrounds, histories, races, languages, and ethnicity can reach their highest potential and participate fully in the economic and social mainstream of society.

We shall adopt as our own the very traits embodied in Tiger Woods: courage, creativity, work ethic, tenacity, integrity, heart, self-esteem, and drive for excellence.

The Foundation will actively encourage and promote parental responsibility and involvement in the lives of children and celebrate the spirit of inclusion in all aspects of human existence.

The Foundation will work to achieve its objectives in a number of ways. These include: recognizing the family as the basic, most important unit in society and identifying the role of the parent as the most important teacher in the life of any child. We shall conduct golf clinics in major metropolitan areas in the U.S. for young people historically denied access and exposure to the sport, support programs that promote educational achievement and job opportunities for inner-city and other disadvantaged youth, and participate in programs and events that promote racial harmony and help people understand and appreciate the value of inclusiveness.

The Tiger Woods Foundation is a 501 (C) 3 non-profit organization (Federal ID# 06-1468499). If you'd like to make a donation to help support our activities, please send a check payable to:

TIGER WOODS FOUNDATION, INC.
P.O. Box 550
Reynoldsburg, OH 43068-0550